To Cling With All Her Heart to Him

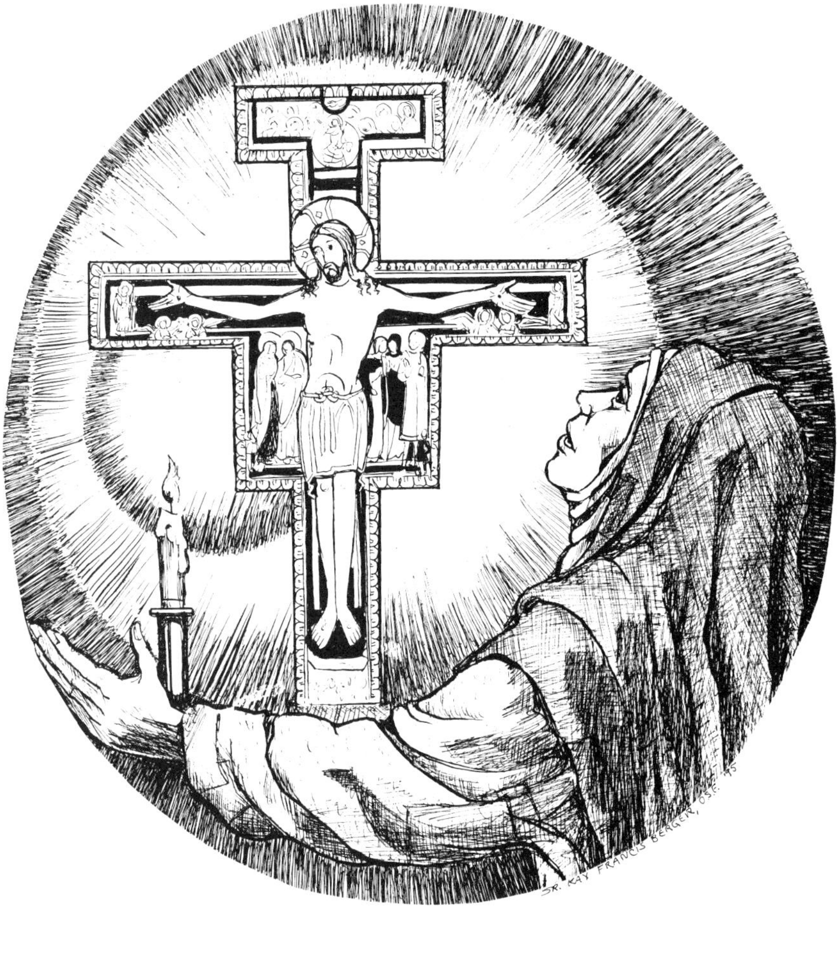

To Cling With All Her Heart to Him

The Spirituality of St. Clare of Assisi

Benet A. Fonck, OFM

Franciscan Press

To Cling With All Her Heart to Him:
   The Spirituality of St. Clare of Assisi
Benet A. Fonck, OFM

Franciscan Press
Quincy University
1800 College Avenue
Quincy, IL 62301
217.228.5670
FAX 217.228.5672

© 1996 Franciscan Press

All rights reserved.

Book design by Laurel Fitch, Chicago, Il.
Cover and book drawings by Sister Kay Frances Berger, OSF

Printed in the United States of America
First Printing: June 1996
1 2 3 4 5 6 7 8 9 0

Library of Congress Cataloging-in-Publication Data
   Fonck, Benet A.
      "To cling with all her heart to Him" : the spirituality of St. Clare of
   Assisi / Benet A. Fonck.
         p.   cm.
      Includes bibliographical references and index.
      ISBN: 0-8199-0973-4 (pbk. : alk. paper)
      1. Clare, of Assisi, Saint. 1194-1253. 2. Spirituality--Catholic Church-
   -History. 3. Catholic Church--Doctrines--History.
   I. Title.
   BX4700.C6F66 1996
   248--dc20   96-16339
                                                            CIP

Permissions
Quotations from the writings of St. Clare of Assisi are taken from *Francis and Clare: The Complete Works*, Regis J. Armstrong and Ignatius Brady, trans. and ed., in *The Classics of Western Spirituality* series (New York: Paulist Press, 1982). Used by permission.

*To all my Poor Clare Sisters
around the world
who teach me constantly how to
gaze upon Jesus,
consider Jesus,
contemplate Jesus,
as I desire to imitate Jesus (cf. 2L20).*

Contents

Introduction   ix

chapter one
"Whose Beauty All the Heavenly Hosts Admire Unceasingly"   3

chapter two
"Whose Love Inflames Our Love"   7

chapter three
"Whose Contemplation is Our Refreshment"   27

chapter four
"Whose Graciousness is Our Joy"   39

chapter five
"Whose Gentleness Fills Us to Overflowing"   49

chapter six
"Models and Mirrors for Others"   61

Endnotes
    78

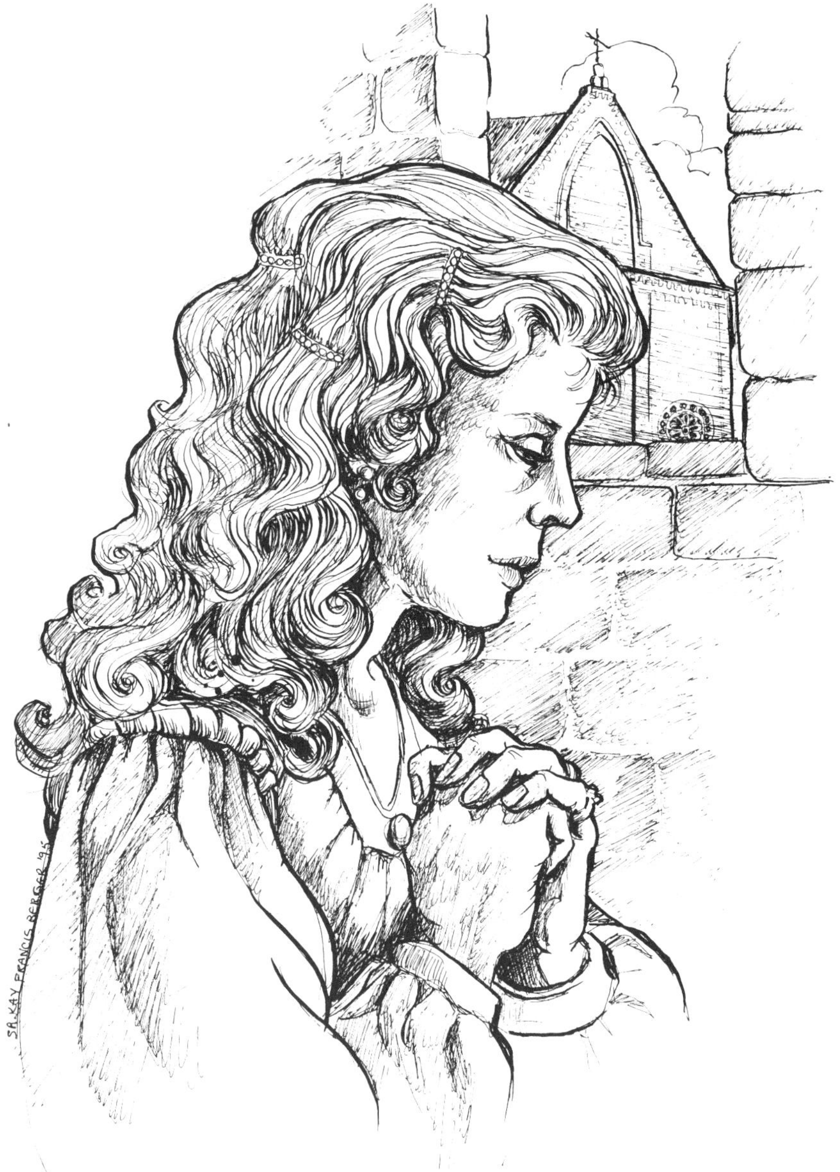
SR. KAY FRANCIS BERGER '95

Introduction

The whole worldwide Franciscan Family has concluded its celebration of the 800th anniversary of the birth of St. Clare of Assisi, the co-founder of the Franciscan Movement and mother of the nuns of the Second Order of St. Francis (Poor Clares).

Clare, who calls herself "a handmaid of Christ" and "a little plant of our holy Father Francis" (TC 5, RCl:3)[1], is considered the feminine incarnation of the evangelical life in the Franciscan tradition and the paradigmatic traveling companion and sister pilgrim on the journey toward holiness for the members of this worldwide spiritual family in the Church. For this reason, pursuing an understanding and appreciation of her vision of gospel living and her experience of intimacy with Jesus Christ is not only an appropriate endeavor on the occasion of this anniversary celebration, but it is also a newly discovered necessity in order to deepen our contemporary commitment to observe the Gospel of our Lord Jesus Christ in the spirit of Francis and Clare.

As much as St. Francis, Clare of Assisi is the model, mirror, and mentor of Franciscan living. A mentor, because this woman teaches us in a clear and imitable way how the Spirit of God calls us to live the gospel ideal and how a human person can challenge others to consider the basic values of a Christ-centered life. A mirror, because whoever looks into her writings and reflects on one's own experience in the light of her countenance will discover a reflection of the glory of God and the beauty of human witness. A model, because the person of Clare epitomizes the effective fulfillment of the promptings of the Spirit and the urging of the Gospel to follow in the footprints of the poor and crucified Christ.

Appropriately, then, we honor this great woman of faith, this feminine complement of St. Francis, this special embodiment of the Franciscan ideal with a series of articles reflecting the basic tenets of her spirituality.

The central themes of her relationship with Christ and the values and behaviors emanating from that relationship can be captured in her own words to St. Agnes of Prague (4L9-13):

> Happy indeed is she to whom it is given to
> > share this sacred banquet, to cling with
> > all her heart to Him
> Whose beauty all the heavenly hosts admire
> > unceasingly,
> Whose love inflames our love,
> Whose contemplation is our refreshment,
> Whose graciousness is our joy,
> Whose gentleness fills us to overflowing,
> Whose remembrance brings a gentle light,
> Whose fragrance will revive the dead,
> Whose glorious vision will be the happiness of
> > all the citizens of
> > the heavenly Jerusalem.[2]

These words, I believe, convey in a poetic and affective mode the real-life experience of St. Clare which she stated formally in the beginning of her rule of life: "The form of life ... is this: to observe the holy Gospel of our Lord Jesus Christ, by living in obedience, without anything of one's own, and in chastity" (RC1:1-2).

So, to delineate this spirituality of St. Clare, we will study each line of the quote above separately. Clare of Assisi describes her gospel life as a clinging to the Lord Jesus and a participation in the sacred banquet of the Kingdom in admiration (discernment), in love (conversion, chastity, and constancy), in contemplation, in graciousness (evangelical poverty), in gentleness (union with others), in remembrance (the mirror), in revivification (fragrance of new life), and in the vision of happiness (evangelization).

Benet A. Fonck, OFM

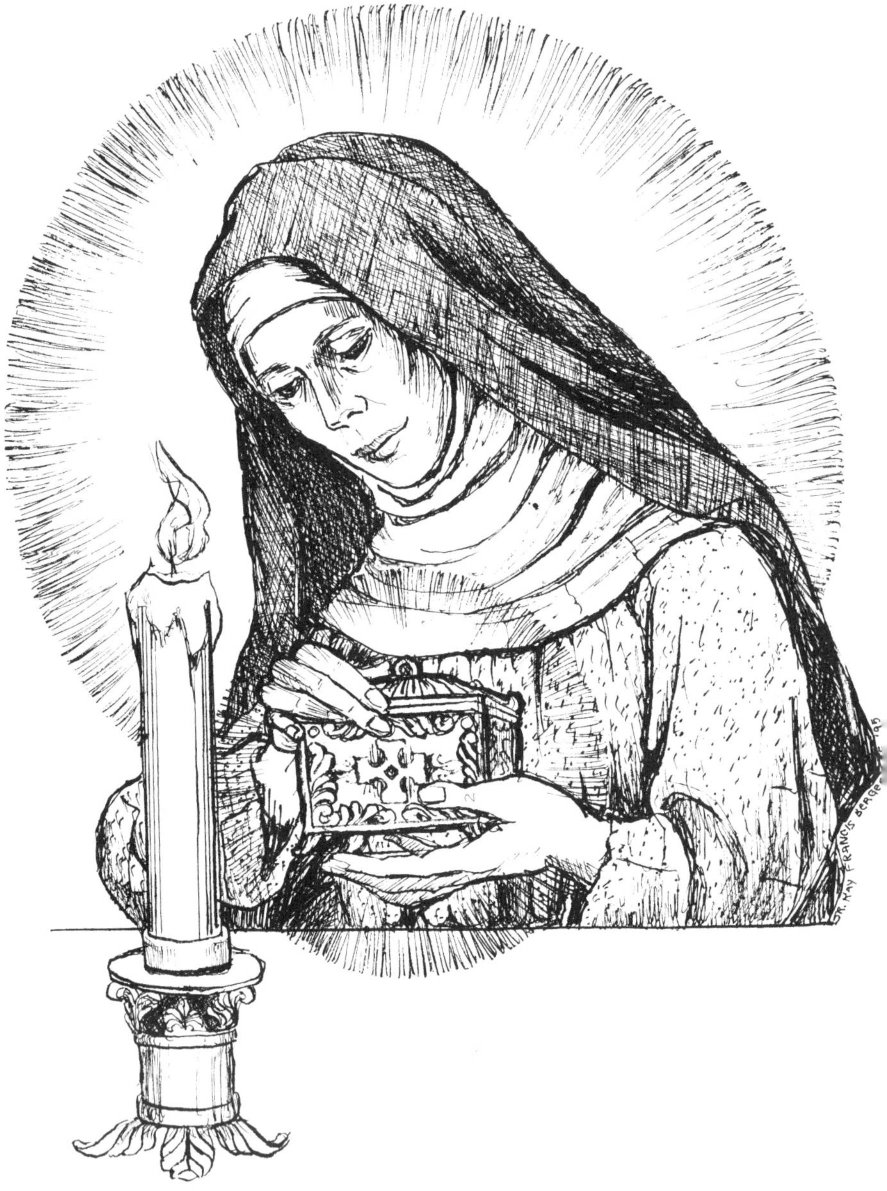

chapter one

"Whose Beauty All the Heavenly Hosts Admire Unceasingly"

For Clare, as for Francis, the gospel life starts with a powerful awareness of being called, being loved, being gifted. It is that wedding of the overwhelming experience of God's gratuitous initiative in her life and the overpowering feeling of absolute emptiness without God. The spiritual journey begins with awesome admiration of God's beauty and, at the very same time, the insatiable passion for discernment or enlightenment.

In her writings St. Clare readily recognizes the prominence of this first step on the spiritual journey toward holiness. She tells Agnes of Prague: "I see that, helped by a special gift of wisdom from the mouth of God Himself and in an awe-inspiring and unexpected way, you have brought to ruin the subtleties of our crafty enemy and the pride that destroys human nature and the vanity that infatuates human hearts" (3L6). And she encourages Ermentrude of Bruges by saying, "Close your ears to the whisperings of hell and bravely oppose its onslaughts. ... Pray and watch at all times. ... Fear not, daughter! God, Who is faithful in all his words and holy in all his deeds, will pour His blessings upon you and your daughters. He will be your help and best comforter for He is our

Redeemer and our eternal reward" (LE6,13,15-16).

The most frequent expression of this admiration of God's inspiration and the willingness to discern the divine initiative is Clare's phrase, "enlightening my heart to do penance" (cf. RC6:1,9:2;TC7). These simple words have a profound dual thrust: confirming the bountiful and merciful gift of God and committing oneself to openness to the guidance of the Spirit.

First of all, with praise and thanksgiving, Clare acknowledges the intervention of the beauty of God's love and mercy and presence: "Among all the other gifts which we have received and continue to receive daily from our benefactor, the Father of mercies, and for which we must express the deepest thanks to our glorious God, our vocation is a great gift. Since it is the more perfect and greater, we should be so much more thankful for it. ... In this, then, we can consider the abundant kindness of God toward us" (TC1,5;cf. also 17).

Because, then, of this gift, it becomes incumbent upon the saint to say to her sisters: "Let them devote themselves to what they must desire to have above all else: the Spirit of the Lord and His holy manner of working, to pray always to Him with a pure heart, and to have humility, patience in difficulty and weakness, and to love those who persecute, blame, and accuse us" (RC10:7).

As a corollary to discernment's dual thrust of gratitude and enlightenment, Clare also highlights the need for discernment with others in community. In this regard she says of St. Francis in her Testament: "Because of [God's] mercy and love, He saw fit to speak these words about vocation and selection through His saint. And our most blessed Father prophesied not only for us, but also for those who were to come to this same holy vocation to which the Lord has called us. ... The Lord has given us the Light of His grace through his holy life and teaching" (TC5,7). To Agnes of Prague she states, "Follow the counsel of our venerable Father, our Brother Elias, the Minister General, so that you may walk more securely in the commands of the Lord" (2L15). In her Rule Clare mandates that the abbess seek the consent of the sisters when admitting novices (RC2:1), consult with her sisters in chapter (RC4:11-13), and have a council of discernment, i.e., "discreets" (RC4:17); that the sisters speak with a discerning spirit in the infirmary regarding the sick; and that the obstinate sister discern the way of penance (RC5:4).

The beginning of the spiritual life for St. Clare is *discernment*, that process of discovery of how the "Father of mercies" is constantly calling her to a new and more abundant life, how the Word-made-flesh is effectively penetrating her everyday existence and making all things new again, how the Spirit is creatively active in her journey toward holiness. This discernment is both that "aha!" experience of realizing how much God loves her, how intensely God calls her, how abundantly God gifts her, and how thoroughly God orders the direction of her journey; and also that docility to place herself at the disposal of the Spirit, that utter malleability to the Potter's clay, that openness and sensitivity to let the Word of God become the "two-edged sword" which cuts to the very marrow of her being. Discernment is gratefully acknowledging God's presence, intuiting God's plan through a specific process of discovery (inner awareness, plus dialogue with others, plus confirmation of a higher authority), and surrendering to God's power.

The process of discernment leads to the passion of returning the love received which is embodied in continual conversion ("penance"), chastity, and constancy. This love-life is sustained by contemplation, poverty, and community. It reaches out of itself to others by mirroring the reality of that love, by sharing the fruits of that spiritual life, and by communicating the vision of gospel life.

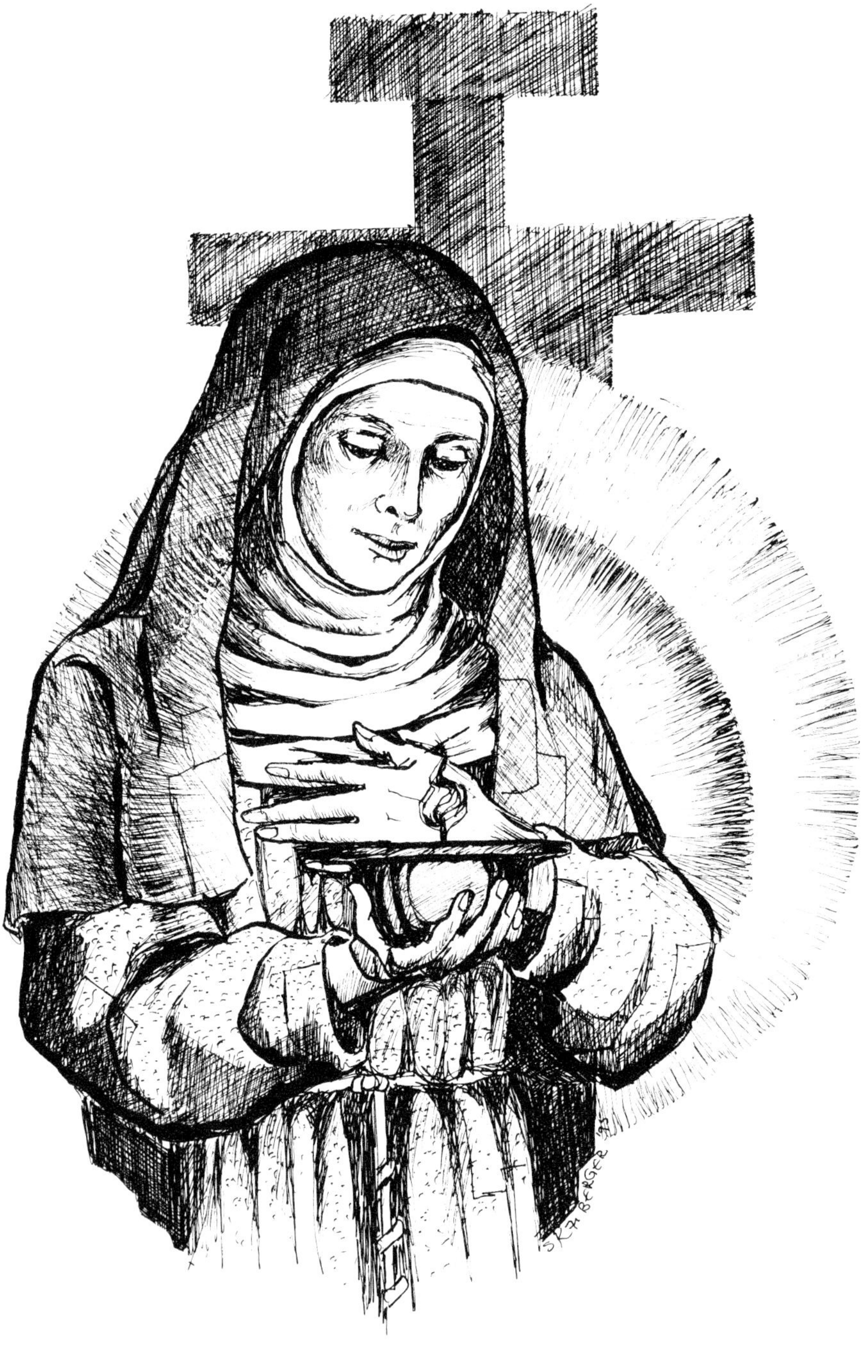

chapter two

"Whose Love Inflames Our Love"

"Observing the holy Gospel" in the Franciscan tradition means developing a relationship of intimacy with the poor and crucified Christ, that particular aspect of the Lord Jesus' presence which was the point of attraction, the constant stimulus, and the ultimate fulfillment for both Francis and Clare. It is coming to know the Way, the Truth, and the Life primarily through the Scriptures; encountering the Beloved through the sacraments and sacramentals of life; taking on or imitating the values, teachings, example, footsteps of the One who loves us. Gospel living is returning the love we've experienced.

Clare of Assisi centered her life on this reality. Her relationship with the Lord Jesus became the source, the end, and the energy for her whole existence. This espousal to the Lord was that overwhelming experience which colored her own spiritual development, her formation of her religious community, and her guidance for others.

Her own words to Agnes of Assisi can be directed to Clare herself: "As someone zealous for the holiest poverty, in the spirit of great humility, and the most ardent charity, you have held fast to the footprints of Him to Whom you have merited to be joined as a Spouse" (2L7), and so "you may sing a new song with the other most holy virgins before the throne of God and of the Lamb and follow the Lamb wherever He may go" (4L3; cf. Rev 14:3-4). Francis himself says of the Poor Ladies of Assisi: "By divine inspiration you have made yourselves daughters and servants of the Most High King, the heavenly Father, and have taken the Holy Spirit as your spouse, choosing to live according to the perfection of the holy Gospel" (RC6:2). In her Testament Clare affirms, "The Son of God became for us the Way which our Blessed Father Francis, His true lover and imitator, has shown and taught us by word and example" (TC2).

This intense love between Clare and her God didn't just happen; it was discovered and developed. History shows that this noble woman had a strong God-orientation throughout her earliest years. Moreover, the experiences of her entrance into a professed evangelical life (especially receiving the palm from Bishop Guido of Assisi, leaving home stealthily through the "door of death" in the dark of night, and joining the brothers at the Portiuncula when she was tonsured and clothed with the habit, cord, and veil) awakened in her an insatiable passion for intimacy with Jesus Christ. Still, Clare knew too well that this flame of love must be continually enkindled by means of a life of continual conversion ("penance"), chastity, and constancy.

Continual Conversion (Penance):

Clare readily stressed the necessity of a life of penance or ongoing conversion for faithful gospel living. In fact, she states that she was enlightened to "do penance" (RC6:1,9:2;TC7).

> She says to Agnes of Prague, the would-be Queen of Bohemia:
> Since you have cast aside all those things which, in this deceitful and turbulent world,

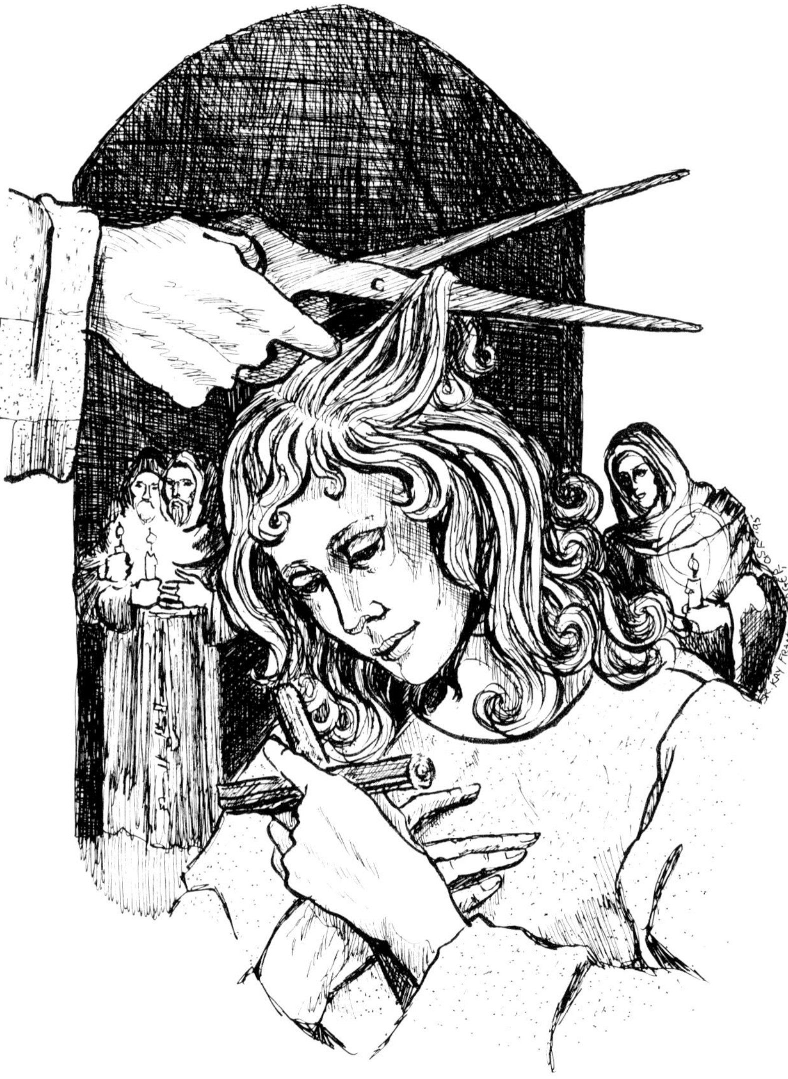
SR. KAY FRANCIS BERGER, OSF '95

ensnare their blind lovers, love Him totally Who gave Himself totally for Your love (3L15).

This is the perfection which will prompt the King Himself to take you to Himself in the heavenly bridal chamber where He is seated in glory on a starry throne because you have despised the splendor of an earthly kingdom and considered of little value the offer of an imperial marriage (2L5-6).

I rejoice and exult with you in the joy of the Spirit, O bride of Christ, because, since you have totally abandoned the vanities of this world, like another most holy virgin, Saint Agnes, you have been marvelously espoused to the spotless Lamb Who takes away the sins of the world (4L7-8).

In her Rule and in her Testament Clare indicates that "penance" is the fundamental first step in the spiritual journey of gospel living which has been activated by the enlightenment of the Holy Spirit. It is the fruit of discernment and the beginning of an intimate and intense relationship with the Blessed Trinity.

We look to the writings of St. Francis to understand the concept of continual conversion or penance which Clare embraced. The beginning of "The First Version of the Letter to the Faithful: Exhortation to the Brothers and Sisters of Penance" outlines the Franciscan Plan of Penance:

> All those who love the Lord with their whole heart, with their whole soul and mind, with their whole strength and love their neighbors as themselves and hate their bodies with their vices and sins, and receive the Body and Blood of our Lord Jesus Christ, and produce worthy fruits of penance: Oh, how happy and blessed

are these men and women when they do these things and persevere in doing them (1-5).

The first step of a life of penance in the Franciscan tradition is to *choose life*: to choose the health or the growth or the life-style that is the way of the loving God for us and thereby return the love God has shown us. This is why Francis begins the first version of the Letter to All the Faithful by calling on "[a]ll those who love the Lord with their whole heart, with their whole soul and mind, with their whole strength, and love their neighbors as themselves" to embark upon a life of penance. In other words, to quote Deuteronomy, "Choose life, then, that you and your descendants may live, by loving the Lord, your God, heeding his voice, and holding fast to him" (30:19). Penance is primarily a positive experience: choosing spiritual health, mental health, emotional health, physical health, and social health as *the* way of returning the love God has bestowed upon us. It is setting oneself on a five-point program of daily living which fulfills God's plan for a healthy, productive, stimulating, creative love-life with him. It is the conscious, concerted effort to work toward well-being of the spirit, mind, emotions, body, and social interactions in order to be open to intimacy with God.

To achieve this end, then, another step is necessary: "hate their bodies with their vices and sins." This is the process of putting aside every encumbrance which hinders growth and instead to *choose to identify with the poor and crucified Christ*. The cross is both death-dealing and life-giving, painfully destructive and triumphantly salvific. So, we choose to put to death (i.e., work to eliminate) those intentions and behaviors which obstruct life and to "hate" (i.e., turn our back on) those human tendencies which detour our loving response to God's initiative of love. As Jesus says in the Gospel of Luke, "Whoever wishes to be my follower must deny one's very self, take up the cross each day, and follow in my steps" (9:23), or, as St. Paul said, "Those who belong to

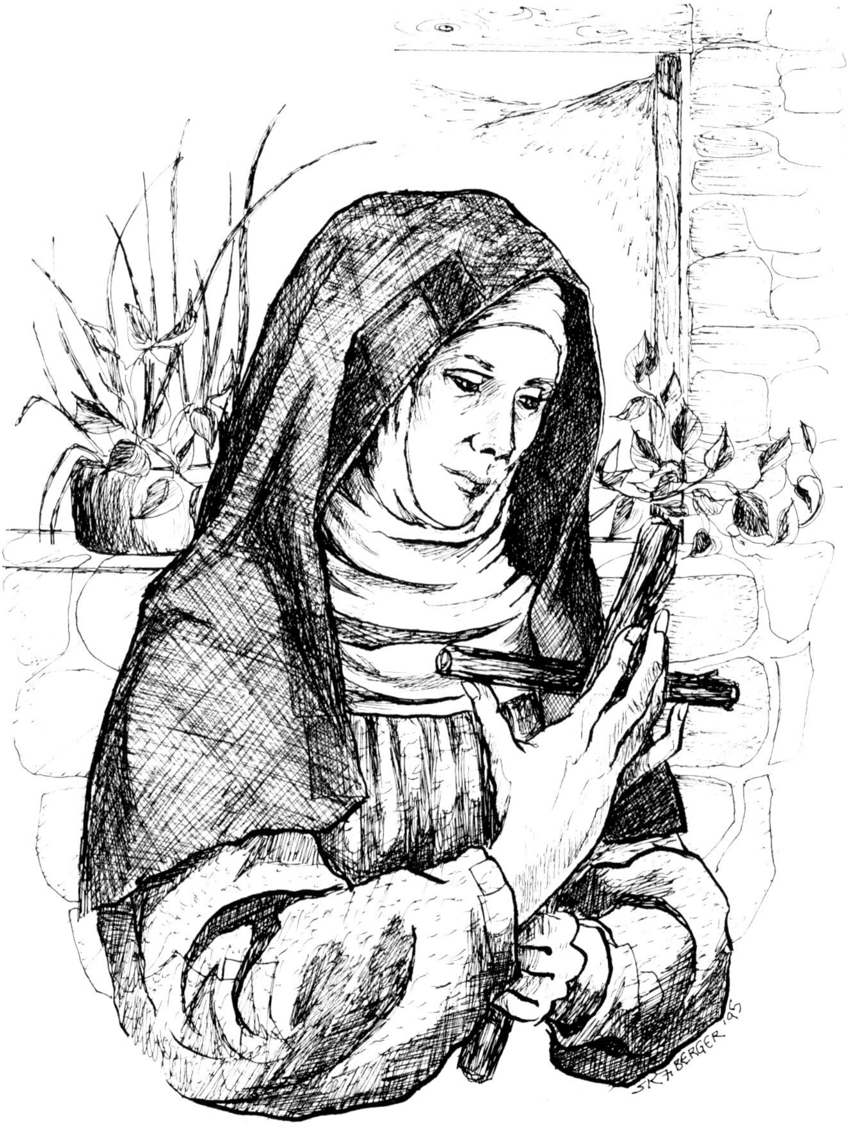

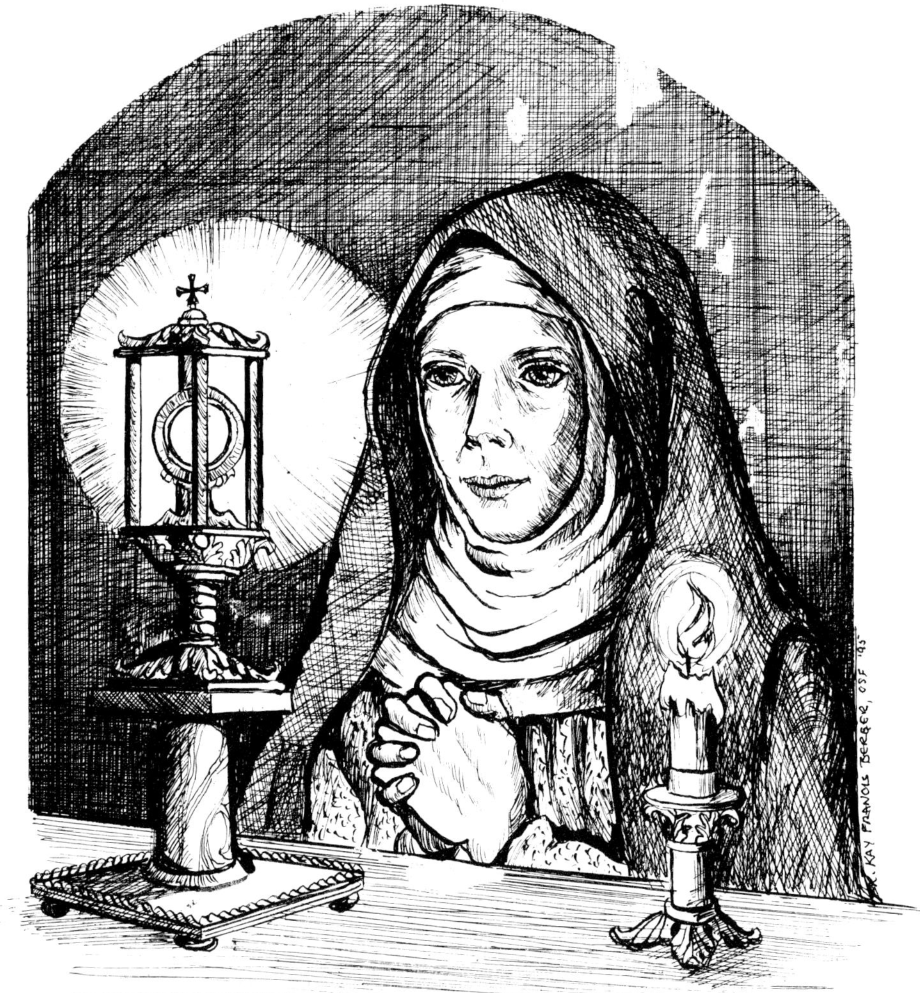
K. KAY FRANCIS BERGER, OSF '95

Christ have crucified their flesh with its passions and desires" (Gal 5:24). The way of the cross is equivalent to the choice to change attitudes and actions which are stumbling blocks to the five areas of health or growth (body, emotions, mind, relationships, and soul), to transform negative events of life (like personal suffering, natural calamities, moral depravity, social injustice, etc.) into positive experiences of the grace of God, to share in sacrificial service (Is 58:6-7) and redemptive suffering (Col 1:24) for the building up of the Body of Christ, and to embrace penitential practices for the sake of fortification or purification.

Thirdly, the plan of penance or ongoing conversion involves the *choice of participating fully in the Eucharist* so that the Body of Christ — Head and members — will become the main source of support and accountability for one's decision to bring renewal through the cross: "and receive the Body and Blood of our Lord Jesus Christ." The Eucharist as covenant, sacrifice, meal, celebration, community-builder, reconciliation, and life-style is the primary experience of the intimate Real Presence to activate and actualize the union between the penitential person and the loving Lord. The "do this in memory of me" of the Eucharist had a special application for Clare who took literally Christ's foot-washing command, "What I just did was to give you an example: as I have done, so you must do" (Jn 13:15); her outreach of self-emptying charity was her personal testimony and her proclamation of a eucharistic lifestyle and hence of an ongoing celebration of Eucharist, for to celebrate is to make present, to make present is to activate, to activate is to make effective. For Clare the Eucharist, then, was both liturgical rite and social responsibility.

Finally, the plan of penance shows its authenticity and its durability in producing "worthy fruits of penance"; in other words, *choosing acts of charity* which share with others the love we've received and thereby make us "mothers [of Christ] when we carry Him in our hearts and body through divine love and a pure and sincere conscience and when we give birth to him through His holy manner of working which should shine before others as an example" (1 Let. to the Faithful, 10).

It is this process of penance which Clare found as the primary means to have Christ's love inflame her love and to embark upon a gospel life.

Chastity:

As a deeply passionate woman whose humanness became a primary vehicle for her intimacy with Jesus, Clare had a special appreciation for chastity as the way to demonstrate and make real that intense love within her which was inflamed by Love eternal. Clare describes this chastity to Agnes of Prague in these words:

> When You have loved Him, You shall be chaste; when You have touched Him, You shall become pure; when you have accepted Him, You shall be a virgin.
> Whose power is stronger,
> Whose generosity is more abundant,
> Whose appearance more beautiful,
> Whose love more tender,
> Whose courtesy more gracious.
> In Whose embrace You are already caught up;
> Who has adorned Your breast with precious stones
> And has placed priceless pearls in Your ears and has surrounded You with sparkling gems as though blossoms of springtime and placed on Your head a golden crown as a sign to all of Your holiness (1L8-11).

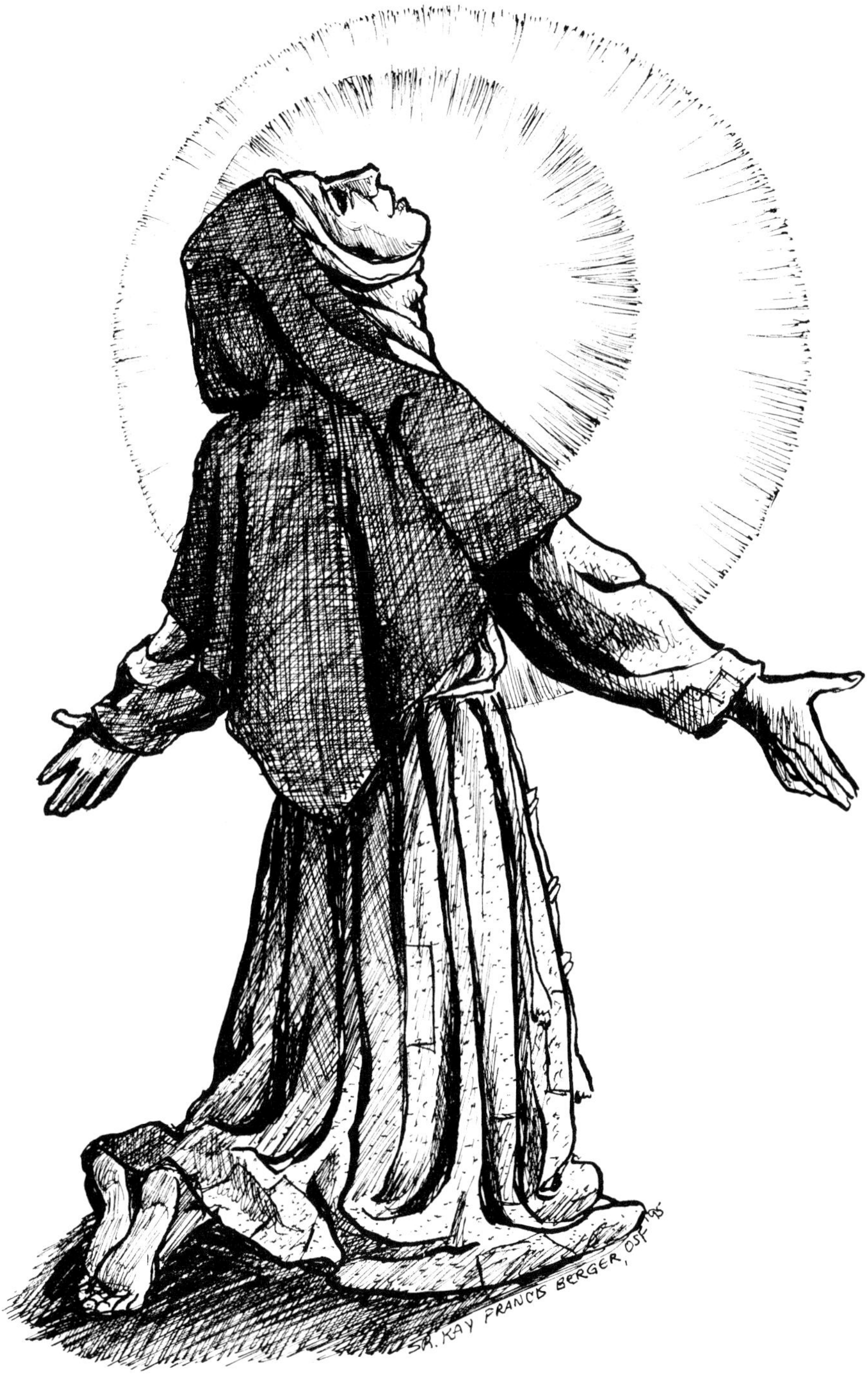
SR. KAY FRANCIS BERGER, OSF

And Clare goes on to say, "Therefore, most beloved sister, or should I say, Lady worthy of great respect: because You are the spouse and the mother and the sister of my Lord Jesus Christ and have been adorned resplendently with the sign of inviolable virginity and most holy poverty: Be strengthened in the holy service which you have undertaken out of an ardent desire for the Poor Crucified" (1L12-13).

For Clare chastity is neither a virtue nor a discipline. Rather, it is a way of acting, a way of expressing one's humanity, a way of life. Celibate chastity, like penance, is foremost the *positive* reality of achieving a profound and passionate intimacy with the Lover who pursues her, and not just the negative "giving up" or deprivation of genital satisfaction or physical parenthood. It is the insatiable desire to dedicate all one's spirit, all one's mind, all one's emotions, all one's body, all one's social interaction to make this relationship happen.

Another aspect of this chastity is summarized in the psalm prayer for Psalm 18, as found in the Liturgy of the Hours:

> Lord God, our strength and our salvation, put
> in us the flame of Your love and make our love
> for You grow to a perfect love which reaches
> to our neighbor.

Not only is chastity directed toward a relationship with the Holy Trinity, but it also determines a new way of relating closely with others without hidden agendas, controlling expectations, or unrealistic demands. Chastity engenders tenderness and affection, compassion and understanding, respect and courtesy, solicitude and attentiveness. It is fostered and called to accountability by life in community — not just a living under one roof, but the investment of one's heart in the heart of another, so that "all may be one" (Jn 17:21) in order to give witness to the presence and power of the divine Lover.

Constancy:

St. Clare's love inflamed by Love is initiated by ongoing conversion, is shaped by celibate chastity, and is maintained by an even constancy, that faithfulness and that authenticity of character which brings about a dedicated perseverance. Very often in her writings she speaks in glowing terms about this necessary quality of the spiritual life:

> With what solicitude and fervor of mind and body, therefore, must we keep the commandments of our God and Father, so that, with the help of the Lord, we may return to Him an increase of his talents (TC6).

> Always be lovers of God and your souls and the souls of your Sisters, and always be eager to observe what you have promised the Lord (BC12).

Perhaps Clare's most beautiful words on constancy appear in her second letter to her "penpal" St. Agnes of Prague:

> Because one thing alone is necessary, I bear witness to that one thing and encourage you, for love of Him to Whom you have offered yourself as a holy and pleasing sacrifice, that, like another Rachel, you always remember your resolution and be conscious of how you began.
> What you hold, may you always hold.
> What you do, may you always do and
>   never abandon.

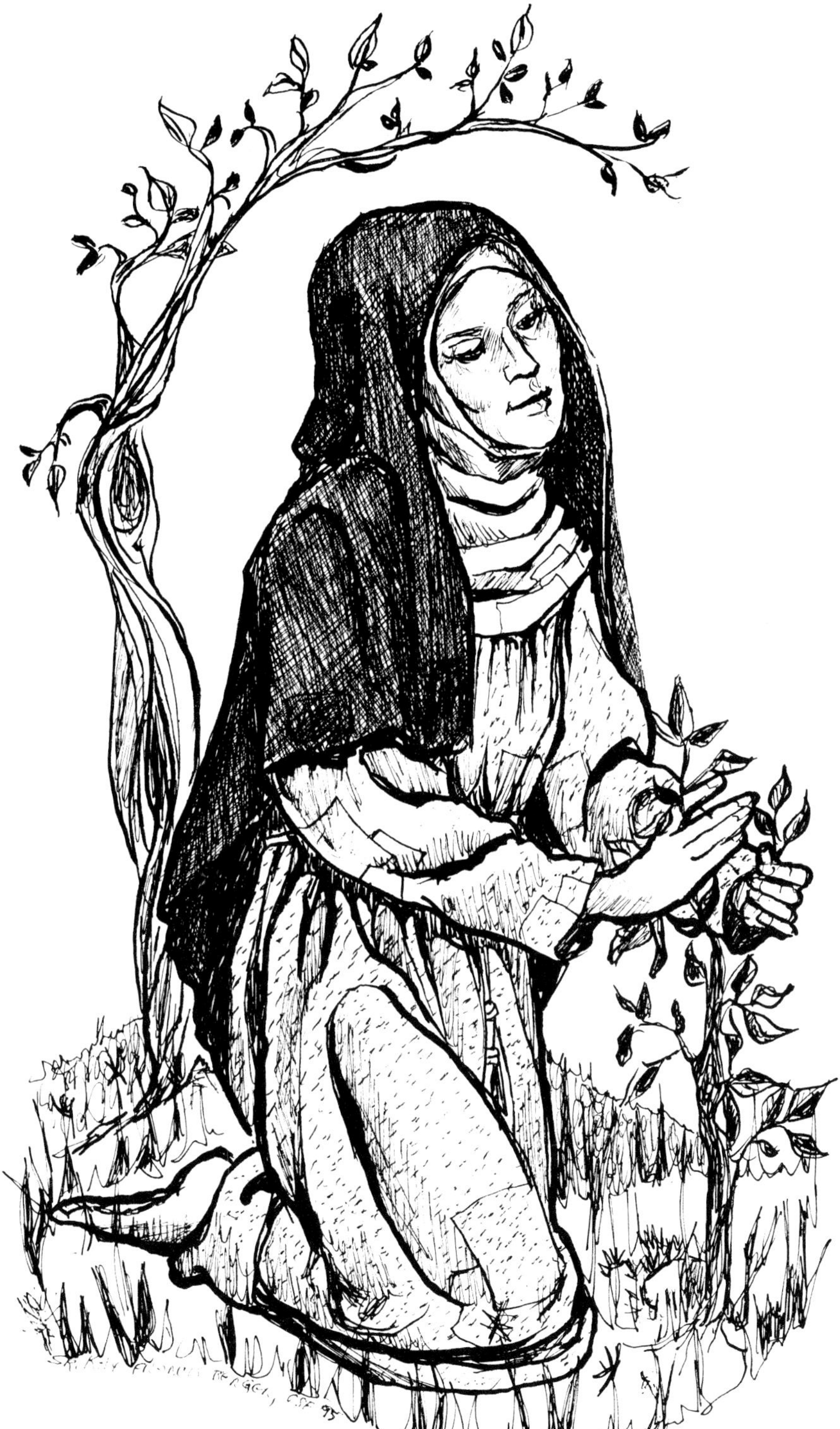

> But with swift pace, light step, and
>   unswerving feet,
> so that even your steps stir up no dust,
> go forward securely, joyfully, and swiftly,
> on the path of prudent happiness,
> believing nothing, agreeing with nothing,
> which would dissuade you from this
>   resolution
> or which would place a stumbling block for
>   you on the way,
> so that you may offer your vows to the
>   Most High
> in the pursuit of perfection
> to which the Spirit of the Lord has called
>   you (2L10-14).

She goes on to say:

> If you suffer with Him, you shall reign with Him,
>   if you weep with Him, you shall rejoice with Him:
>   if you die with Him on the cross of tribulation,
>   you shall possess heavenly mansions
>   in the splendor of the saints,
>   and, in the Book of Life, your name shall be called
>   glorious among all (2L21-22).

This constancy is the direct result of penance and chastity and is the moral equivalent of the indissolubility of marriage vows: "[S]o that He Whom you serve with the total desire of your soul may bestow on you the reward for which you long" (1L32), [r]emain faithful until death, dearly beloved, to Him to Whom you have promised yourself, for you shall be crowned by Him with the garland of life" (LE4).

The life-program to maintain this constancy is the sustaining force of contemplation, poverty, and togetherness and the outreach efforts of mirroring Christ, sharing the fruits of new life, and witnessing to a vision of happiness.

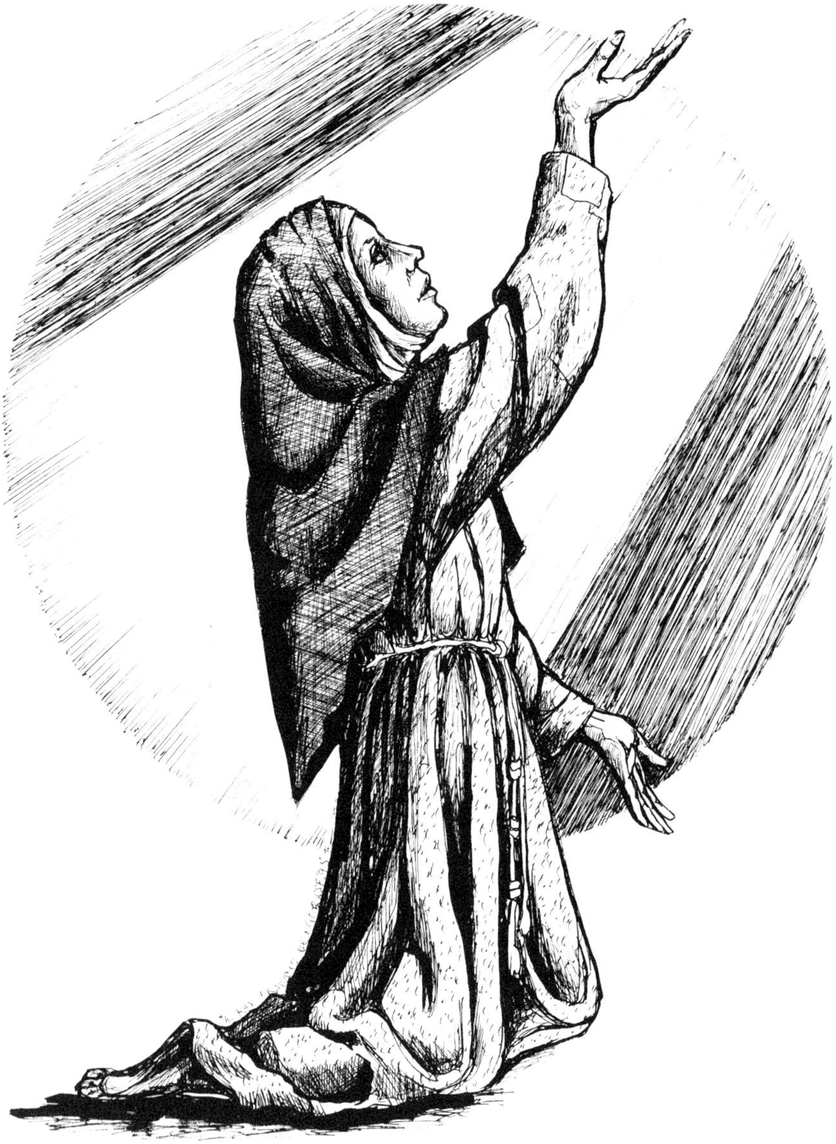

chapter three

"Whose Contemplation Is Our Refreshment"

For Clare of Assisi contemplation was refreshment: making fresh again her intimacy with the Lord Jesus which brought rejuvenation, revitalization, reinvigoration, and renewal to her own self-awareness, to her life with her sisters, and to her presence to the world, so that she could "attain the glory of everlasting happiness" (1L2). She experienced contemplation as that peace-filled enjoyment of her intimate relationship with the Blessed Trinity and the means to live more intensely the gospel life she embraced after the example and inspiration of St. Francis. The contemplative experience is a credible sign of being rooted in Christ and an ongoing source for realizing that passionate, affective, and refreshing oneness with God.

While the life of contemplation was central to her whole spirituality, integral for maintaining her life of penance, chastity, and fidelity, and necessary for keeping alive the spirit of discernment, Clare only spoke succinctly, yet dramatically, about this important dimension of living:

> As you contemplate further His ineffable delights, eternal riches and honors, and sigh for them in the great desire and love of your

heart, may you cry out:
> Draw me after You!
> We will run in the fragrance of Your
>   perfumes, O heavenly Spouse!
> I will run and not tire,
> until You bring me into the wine-cellar,
> until Your left hand is under my head
> and Your right hand will embrace me
>   happily
> and you will kiss me with the happiest
>   kisses of your mouth (4L28-32).

Contemplation for Clare is that intimate and all-encompassing encounter with the person of God. It is an experience that is both given and received, initiated and accepted, infused and acquired: the gift of God to make himself present in an intense way, and the developed practice of recognizing and responding to this intense presence.

The contemplative journey embraces a whole hierarchy of experiences, sometimes present together, sometimes quite separate from each other: ecstacy or rapture, abiding peace and surety, fleeting intensity, an ongoing comfort factor to live easily and work productively in his presence, the "winter" or "dark night" of the soul.

This reality embodies all the qualities of a powerful and passionate relationship between the lover and the beloved. Woven together are the precious threads of the satiation of senses, the hunger or thirst to maintain encounter, the experience of inner fulfillment (meaning, serenity, union), the willingness to trust and submit to the other's will without losing one's own freedom, the openness to ask lovingly for what one needs, the longing for total self-giving, wanting the complete happiness of the other while desiring to take on and be motivated by the good of the other, the ability to see life from the other's point of view.

Contemplation has a sacramental quality to it because

it both expresses concretely and brings about effectively that oneness between the human person and the Blessed Trinity which throughout Sacred Scripture is described as the goal of existence. While it is a means involving all the senses to intensify and develop this intense relationship, it is also a sign that the inner reality of union already exists. As an instrument for bringing about intimacy and belonging, it reflects the reality of God's person and one's own person interacting. Contemplation is "here" but "not yet": it is that peace-filled enjoyment of one's unity with God, and the way to achieve the fullness of an experience still maturing.

To maintain the efficacy of contemplation as a means to an end and as a statement of actuality, certain qualities of life have to be present both interiorly and exteriorly. On the inside, a person has to be committed to an ongoing change of heart, to be willing to embrace personal discipline, to approach prayer as a conscious unitive experience and not just devotional or intercessory, to experiment with various techniques of centering or focusing, and to experience work as a grace or gift ("The sisters to whom the Lord has given the grace of working are to work faithfully and devotedly. ... They must do this in such a way that, while they banish idleness, the enemy of the soul, they do not extinguish the Spirit of holy prayer and devotion to which all other things of our earthly existence must contribute" (RC7:1,2). The environment or ambience in which a contemplative person lives must also contribute to the experience. There has to be a contained or focused "state of the heart" which concentrates one's attention on the loving reality of interactive presence. The cloister and the quiet life are both signs and means of this concentration, and in the Rule of Clare (chapters 5 and 11) these provide a framework for the other two exterior characteristics for contemplation; namely, the mutual support and group spiritual direction of community life and the simple "unclutteredness" of gospel poverty. Imagine, then, the contemplative experience as a fine painting of blended colors (the interior qualities) depicting union, matted with the complementary hues of mutuality and simplicity, and framed in a highlighted way with silence and cloister.

Contemplation has three goals: to make evident and to make happen a) the knowing of God intimately, b) self-knowledge in God's presence, and c) life with God before the world.

The first goal is *to know, encounter, and identify with the person of Jesus Christ and his saving love for us.* St. Clare captured beautifully this meaning and methodology of contemplation when she said to Agnes of Prague: "O most noble Queen, gaze upon Him, consider Him, contemplate Him, as you desire to imitate Him" (2L20). She expressed the development of true affective prayer in the Franciscan tradition:

a) gazing upon the poor and crucified Christ, looking deeply into his countenance, coming to understand his words and his actions, knowing the person of God (Father, Son, and Spirit; Creator, Redeemer, Sanctifier; Mercy, Love, Energy, etc.);

b) considering the reality of God, encountering the God who loves, praising God for being, thanking God for doing;

c) contemplating this loving God, entering into union with the Divine, investing the whole of one's physical and psychic and spiritual energy into this relationship;

d) imitating this God, making the values and teachings of the Word made flesh one's own, assuming the life-direction and the example of this God in human form.

The self-giving of this level of contemplation brings about healing, reconciliation, and peace to the person who embarks upon this journey.

Moreover, this first goal of contemplation also implies coming to know, encounter, and identify with the redemptive qualities of the saving Lord: poverty, humility, charity. As Clare begs Agnes of Prague:

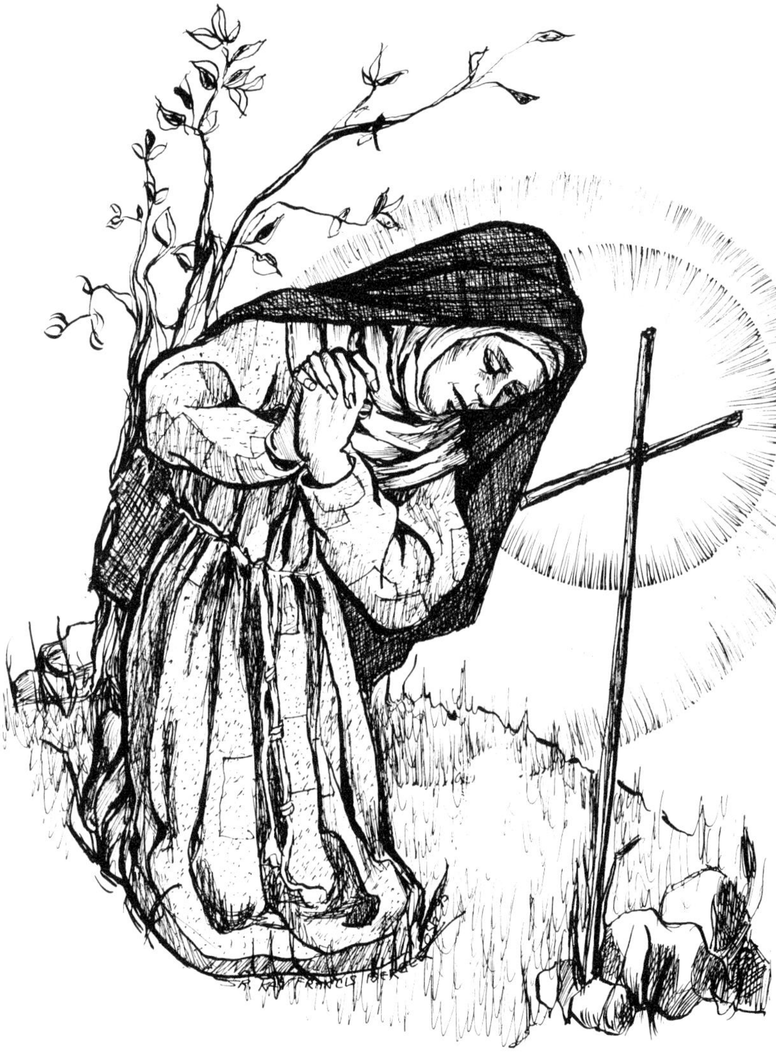

> Look upon Him Who became contemptible for you, and follow Him, making Yourself contemptible in the world for Him. Your Spouse, though more beautiful than the children of men, became, for your salvation, the lowest of men, despised, struck, scourged untold times throughout His whole body, and then died amid the sufferings of the Cross (2L19-20).

In like manner she says to Ermentrude of Bruges:

> O dearest one, look up to heaven which calls us on, and take up the Cross and follow Christ Who has gone on before us: for through Him we shall enter into His glory after many and diverse tribulations. Love God from the depths of your heart and Jesus, His Son, Who was crucified for us sinners. Never let the thought of Him leave your mind but meditate constantly on the mysteries of the Cross and the anguish of His mother as she stood beneath the Cross (LE9-12).

This aspect of contemplation heightens one's awareness of how much we are loved and why and provides the intuition and the awesome wonder necessary for making union happen.

A third dimension of this first goal is to know, encounter, and identify with the reign of God in one's life, for, if a person experiences who God is and what God has done and how God has entered into intimacy with her or him, then the awareness of and dedication to the dominion of God is an automatic conclusion. Within, there is the experience of the kingdom of truth and light; without, it is being able to see, to be a part of, and to long to achieve a kingdom of justice, love, and peace (cf. the Preface for the Solemnity of Christ the King).

The second goal of the contemplative life is *to know oneself in the light of God's presence and revelation.* This self-knowledge has various dimensions which are sewn together like a patchwork quilt that gives warmth and comfort and consolation to human existence:

a) The willingness to acknowledge and fulfill one's human desire for union, ecstacy, intimacy, and belonging gives a person the courage to be drawn to the Lord and the eagerness to move toward the Lord. It is a posture of openness and of longing.

b) The need for a person in love to take to oneself the ups and downs of the beloved's experiences and to lend the power of his or her psychic or spiritual or physical energy to uplift the beloved leads to the decision to identify with the poor and crucified Christ in his passion, death, and resurrection. Moreover, in the development of authentic intimacy, whatever was the point of attraction in a relationship becomes the source of energy for pursuing that relationship and the means to complete the oneness sought; for Francis and Clare, the poor and crucified Christ was the point of attraction, the source of energy, and the experience of ecstatic fulfillment.

c) When the contemplative strives to assume the values and virtues, the priorities and plans of the Lord, he or she comes in touch with one's level of responsibility to let go of a personal self-centered and self-promoting agenda and to take on an other-directed life. This process is an evaluation of one's own tendencies toward selfishness, egoism, and narcissism and of one's honest commitment to surrender to the Providence of God.

d) The vision of profound and perpetual union which results from contemplation places a person in the position to examine one's efforts to transform his or her own image in the likeness of God and one's actual receptivity of God's treasures. Contemplation is a voyage into utter, naked honesty.

e) The ongoing awareness of God's own fidelity to self-revelation through contemplation and the persevering attentiveness of the contemplative are sure and credible signs of one's forward movement and ongoing development toward holiness. The contemplative experience is a barometer of one's progress in the spiritual life.

The third goal of contemplation is *to become the image and the instrument of the human being's life with God before all the world.* There is an evangelizing quality to the contemplative experience (to be more fully developed in future articles) which opens the eyes and the mind and the heart of the Church and the world to the presence of God.

The contemplative, by her/his very existence and style of prayer, reminds the Church that union is the primary motivation for being the Body of Christ, that unfolding the mysteries of God is the basic posture for ministry, and that the fundamental reason for spiritual striving is to establish the reign of God within at the present time to be completed in eternity in the fullness of the Kingdom.

In regards to secular society and the structures of the world, the person of contemplation gives witness to the fact that there is more to progress than science and technology, more to wealth than possessions and competition, more to interaction than existentialism and subjectivism, more to life than freedom of choice and self-determination. The contemplative also conveys the truth that life has meaning and purpose only with a God-focus; that human activity has direction and fulfillment only when Jesus Christ is the source, end, and energy for living; and that the human heart is intended to be centered on another.

Contemplation, as Clare teaches us by her words and her example, is one of the basic foundation stones for building an authentic gospel life, inspired by discerned enlightenment and shaped by the love which is enfleshed in continual conversion, chastity, and constancy. Together with evangelical poverty and life in community, this grounding of the spiritual life gives rise to the three-fold beacon of evangelization: mirroring God's self-revelation, witnessing to new life, and proclaiming the Good News of salvation.

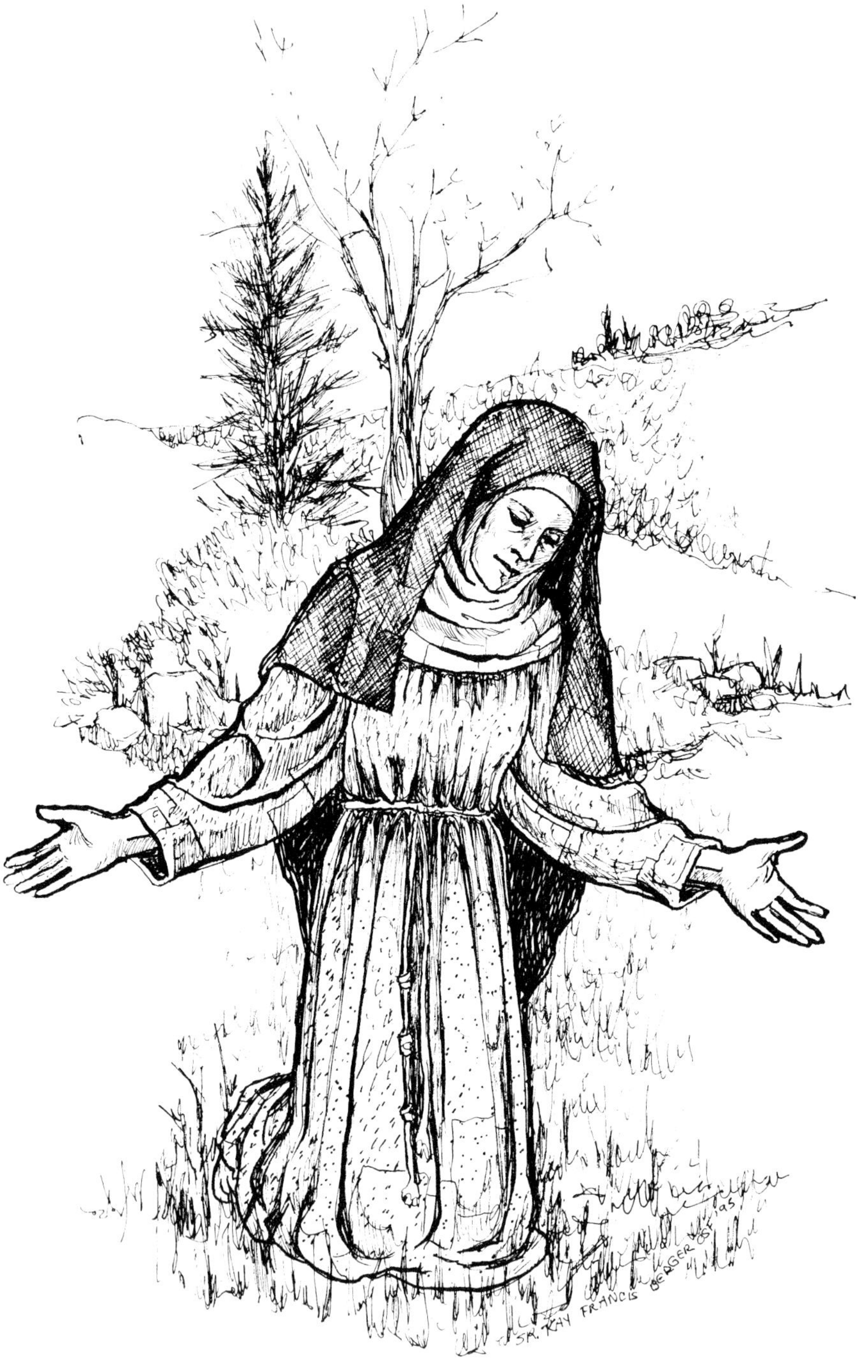
SR. KAY FRANCIS BERGER OSF '95

chapter four

"Whose Graciousness Is Our Joy"

Because of her intense consciousness of God's graciousness and gratuity toward her which became evident through her life of discernment, penance, and contemplation, St. Clare's heart welled up with immense joy. This joy led her to an impassioned response to embrace a life of gospel poverty as an expression of her intimacy with the poor and crucified Christ, of her trust in the Providence of the "Father of mercies," and of her docility to the working of the Holy Spirit.

This hallmark of poverty characterized the complete identity of the "Poor Ladies of San Damiano" (as the Poor Clares were first called) and led to what Clare considered the greatest gift of God's Church to her community, the "privilege of poverty": the right to be compelled by no one to receive any possessions and renounce the desire for all temporal things. Confirmed orally in 1216 by Pope Innocent III, this privilege was confirmed on Sept. 15, 1228, by Pope Gregory IX. The text of this document is significant because it provides a complete summary of St. Clare's approach to the gospel life and the importance of evangelical poverty in that context:

> As is evident, you have renounced the desire for all temporal things, desiring to dedicate

yourselves to the Lord alone. Because of this, since you have sold all things and given them to the poor (Lk 18:22), you propose not to have any possessions whatsoever, clinging in all things to the footprints of Him, the Way, the Truth, and the Life (Jn 14:6), Who, for our sake, was made poor. Nor does a lack of possessions frighten you from a proposal of this sort; for the left hand of the heavenly Spouse is under your head to support the weakness of your body, which you have placed under the law of your soul through an ordered charity. Finally, He Who feeds the birds of the heavens and clothes the lilies of the field will not fail you in either food or clothing, until He ministers to you in heaven, when His right hand especially will more happily embrace you in the fullness of His beatific vision. Therefore, we confirm with our apostolic authority, as you requested, your proposal of most high poverty, granting you by the authority of this letter that no one can compel you to receive possessions. And if any woman does not wish to, or cannot observe a proposal of this sort, let her not have a dwelling place among you, but let her be transferred to another place.

This text is significant not because it is an historical innovation in the life of cloistered religious women, but especially because it characterizes the whole meaning and practice of gospel poverty for Clare and her sisters.

For St. Clare, as with Francis, poverty was not so much a virtue whose practice makes one holy nor even a value to be embraced for its own sake. Poverty was a concrete demonstration of imitating and conforming to and identifying with the poor and crucified Christ: because Christ was poor and because Christ is her Lover and because she strives to be completely one with the Beloved, Clare is poor. Moreover because of the graciousness and gratuity of the God who created her and redeemed her and sanctifies her, she in joy totally surrenders to that God all the possessions of her mind and heart and will and hand in evangelical poverty to be free and open to receive her God fully.

Clare's words about poverty are rich and abundant. Even the formal text of the rule exhibits a wealth of insight and dedication:

> The sisters shall not acquire anything as their own, neither a house nor a place nor anything at all; instead, as pilgrims and strangers in this world who serve the Lord in poverty and humility, let them send confidently for alms. Nor should they feel ashamed, since the Lord made himself poor for us in this world. This is that summit of highest poverty which has established you, my dearest sisters, as heirs and queens of the kingdom of heaven; it has made you poor in the things of this world but has exalted you in virtue. Let this be your portion, which leads you into the land of the living. Dedicating yourselves totally to this, my most beloved sisters, do not wish to have anything else forever under heaven for the name of Our Lord Jesus Christ and His most holy Mother (RC8:1-2).

Time and again in the rule Clare indicates that poverty is the standard for faithful gospel living: "The form of life...is...to observe the holy Gospel...by living in obedience, *without anything of one's own*, and in chastity" (RC1:1-2). "When the year of probation is ended, let her be received into obedience, promising to observe always our life and *form of poverty*" (RC2:8). The profession of this "form of poverty" is also a prerequisite for the election of the abbess (RC4:3 & RC6:4). So central is this reality of gospel poverty which she learned from St. Francis that she quotes his words verbatim in the rule: "I, brother Francis, the little one, wish to follow the life and poverty of our most high Lord Jesus Christ and of His most holy mother and to persevere in this until the end; and I ask and counsel you, my ladies, to live always in this most holy life and in poverty. And keep most careful watch that you never depart from this by reason of the teaching or advice of anyone" (RC6:3).

Clare's most eloquent and ebullient praise of poverty comes in her first letter to Agnes of Prague:

> O blessed poverty, who bestows eternal riches
>   on those who love and embrace her!
> O holy poverty, to those who possess and
>   desire you God promises the kingdom of
>   heaven and offers, indeed, eternal glory
>   and blessed life!
> O God-centered poverty, whom the Lord
>   Jesus Christ
>   Who ruled and now rules heaven
>   and earth,
>   Who spoke and things were made,
>   condescended to embrace before all else!
>   (1L15-17)

> What a great laudable exchange:
>   to leave the things of time for eternity,
>   to choose the things of heaven for the
>   goods of earth,
>   to receive the hundred-fold in place of one,
>   and to possess a blessed and eternal life.
>   (1L30)

Between these two quotes Lady Clare presents a most profound treatise of the meaning and purpose of gospel poverty:

> The foxes have dens, He says, and the birds of the air have nests, but the Son of Man, Christ, has nowhere to lay His head, but bowing His head gave up His spirit.
>
> If so great and good a Lord, then, on coming into the Virgin's womb, chose to appear despised, needy, and poor in this world, so that people who were in utter poverty and want and in absolute need of heavenly nourishment might become rich in Him by possessing the kingdom of heaven, then rejoice and be glad! Be filled with a remarkable happiness and a spiritual joy! Contempt of the world has pleased You more than its honors, poverty more than earthly riches, and You have sought to store up greater treasures in heaven rather than on earth, where rust does not consume nor moth destroy nor thieves break in and steal. Your reward, then, is very great in heaven! And You have truly merited to be called a sister, spouse, and mother of the Son of the Father of the Most High and of the glorious Virgin.
>
> You know, I am sure, that the kingdom of heaven is promised and given by the Lord only to the poor: for he who loves temporal things loses the fruit of love. Such a person cannot serve God and Mammon, for either the one is loved and the other hated, or the one is served and the other despised.

You also know that one who is clothed cannot fight with another who is naked, because he is more quickly thrown who gives his adversary a chance to get hold of him; and that one who lives in the glory of earth cannot rule with Christ in heaven.

Again, you know that it is easier for a camel to pass through the eye of a needle than for a rich man to enter the kingdom of heaven. Therefore, you have cast aside Your garments, that is, earthly riches, so that You might not be overcome by the one fighting against you, and that You might enter the kingdom of heaven through the straight path and the narrow gate (1L18-29).

The purpose of evangelical poverty in the Franciscan-Clarian tradition is threefold: intimacy, trust, and docility—

a) to conform oneself to the self-giving or "kenosis" (self-emptying) of the poor and crucified Christ as a manifestation of and means toward intimacy with him. It is identifying oneself with the words of St. Paul: "For your sake [Christ] made himself poor though he was rich, so that you might become rich by his poverty" (2Cor 8:9).

b) to accept the gift of the kingdom's treasures as a sign of one's trust in God's loving Providence. It is living out Jesus' words in the Gospel of Matthew: "Do not lay up for yourselves an earthly treasure. ... Where your treasure is, there your heart is also" (6:19,21).

c) to open oneself completely to the inspiration and guidance of the Holy Spirit so that a person is docile and receptive to the Paraclete's promptings toward truth, toward holiness, toward peace, toward all possibilities for deeper living. It is making present in one's life the words of Scripture: "Do not stifle the Spirit" (1Thes 5:19), and "When he comes, being the Spirit of Truth, He will lead you to all truth" (Jn 16:13).

The content of this life of poverty is not a virtuous practice nor a social condition, but rather a chosen life-style. It is concretizing in practical, everyday behavior the Beatitudes in which one suffers the loss of a "possession" to gain a treasure. It is the parables of the pearl of great price and the field of great worth played out in everyday existence. As pilgrims and strangers on their way to the Father, those who are evangelically poor are like the lilies of the field or the birds of the air; perhaps it might even be more accurate to say that they are like the ducks of the pond off whose back the water drips so that they can fly to new heights.

Gospel poverty, moreover, is living "without property," which means not having the attachments or appropriations of will or mind or heart or hand or person to bog one down, to distract one's focus, to detour one's striving. It is the choice to simplify one's life (i.e., attend to one's needs, lessen one's wants, and curb one's luxuries) so that neither a person's bullheadedness or closed-mindedness or hard-heartedness or materialistic consumerism or inordinate affections get in the way of centering one's life on relating to God in intimacy, trust, and docility. This style of life is liberating, cleaning out the clutter of one's heart to make room for God to dwell therein, unshackling one's spirit to soar to new heights of spiritual development, removing the distractions of one's mind to concentrate on the presence and power of God, emancipating one's body from the dependency upon unhealthy intake and practices, and unfettering those attachments to other people which keep one tied to the earthly and hold a person in slavery to unproductive and, in fact, destructive relationships.

This evangelical poverty also has a dimension of outreach to it because as human beings we become stewards of the goods received for the benefit of God's children. The "privilege of poverty" in everyday existence has with it a corresponding responsibility: to live in moderation to offset the squandering of consumerism, to demonstrate generosity in order to overcome the hoarding and manipulating of selfishness on all levels of human existence, and to promote justice so as to obviate the enslavement of peoples and structures and nature because of rampant materialism, misuse of power, unconscionable oppression, and unwarranted destruction of the environment.

This is the gospel poverty that Francis and Clare embraced which, together with contemplation and community, incarnated the gospel life born of discernment, formed by penance, chastity, and constancy, and proclaimed by being a mirror, a witness, and a prophet.

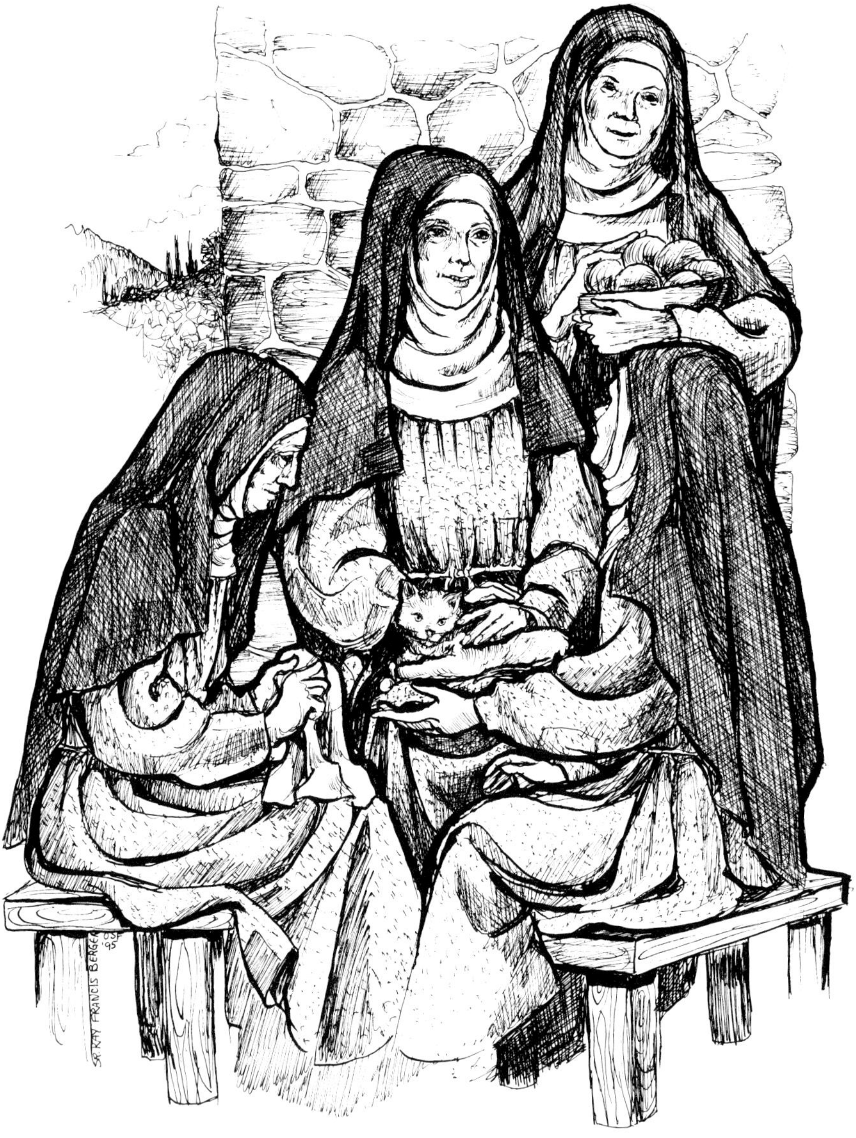
SR. KAY FRANCIS BERGER
'95

chapter five

"Whose Gentleness Fills Us to Overflowing"

The gentleness of God, which filled Clare and her sisters to overflowing and brought them to praise God's magnanimity and kindness in their regard, was not some obtuse category nor some vague quality, but rather it was constant, evident reality seen on the faces of the sisters, witnessed in their love for each other, and realized through their mutual union.

The unanimity of the sisters, "possessing the one love, united in spirit and ideas" (Phil 2:2) was the countenance of God's gentleness, the sacrament of God's tenderness, the witness of God's kindly regard. As Jesus prayed, "that they may be one in us [so] that the world may believe that you sent me" and "that their unity may be complete [so that] the world [may] know ... that you loved them as you love me" and "that your love for me may live in them and I may live in them" (Jn 17:21,23,26), so life in community is meant to both show and secure the gentle, loving, and caring presence of the Most High.

Because of the nature of the enclosed monastery where the Poor Ladies lived, this demand upon their life together was expressed with more clarity and conviction by Clare than by Francis. Whereas Francis experienced fraternity as an essential quality for his brothers' "life on the road" in pursuit of the gospel life (both observing it and proclaiming it), Clare insisted that mutuality and courtesy among the sisters were essential components of the evangelical life itself. One of her particularly precious gifts to the Franciscan Movement was this emphasis upon mutual love which has borne fruit in many kinds of interactive reciprocity among the various components of this worldwide spiritual family.

From Clare's perspective this life in community had a number of specific objectives:

The sisters together in mutual charity are seen as a *means of salvation* in manifesting the profound relationship that exists in the Inner Life of God. Community is seen to be a sacrament of the Divine Community of Love, a sign of the gentleness of the Blessed Trinity itself:

> Let the tongue of the flesh be silent when I seek to express my love for you; and let the tongue of the Spirit speak because the love I have for you, O blessed daughter, can never be fully expressed by the tongue of the flesh, and even what I have written is an inadequate expression (4L35).

Manifesting their love for one another in community expressed and brought about the Love which exists in the Trinity and which is shared with us.

Community is the *binding force of holiness* because it gives meaning, purpose, and expression to our living in contemplation and poverty:

> I admonish and exhort in the Lord Jesus Christ that the sisters be on their guard against all pride, vainglory, envy, greed, worldly care and anxiety, detraction and murmuring, dissention and division. Let them be ever zealous to preserve among themselves the

> unity of mutual love, which is the bond of perfection (RC10:4-5).

Building community provides the environment and the motivation for intimate union with the Lord:

> Loving one another with the charity of Christ, let the love you have in your hearts be shown outwardly in your deeds so that, compelled by such an example, the sisters may always grow in the love of God and in charity for one another (TC18).

Community is meant to be a *visible support system* to sustain and complement the efforts of all the members in striving to attain a meaningful relationship with Christ:

> I sigh with such happiness in the Lord because I know you see that you make up most wonderfully what is lacking both in me and in the other sisters in following the footprints of the poor and humble Jesus Christ (3L4).

Our loving attention, mutual help, and sympathetic understanding for one another supplement our individual particular deficiencies and challenge us to a deeper participation in the life of God.

Another objective of life in community is *to participate in the saving work of God* by sustaining and supporting the weaker members of the Church by our example and efforts; as Clare says, "I consider you a co-worker of God himself and a support of the weak members of his ineffable Body" (3L8). Our prayers of intercession and reparation, our quiet example of love and joy and respect, our witness to the real values of life lift up, inspire, and strengthen those who need or desire this kind of motivation and fortification to live and work as members of the Body of Christ. This mission is particularly important when we consider the powerful effect of a contemplative community upon the local church of a diocese.

Finally, the objective of community is *to give the world an example and a point of reference* for the true values and priorities of human life:

> With what solicitude and fervor of mind and body must we keep the commandments of our God and Father, so that with the help of the Lord, we may return an increase of his talents. For the Lord Himself not only has set us up as an example and mirror for others, but also for our own sisters whom the Lord has called to our own way of life, so that they in turn will be a mirror and example to those living in the world. Since, therefore, the Lord has called us to such great things, that those who are to be models and mirrors for others may behold themselves in us, we are truly bound to praise and bless the Lord and be strengthened constantly in Him to do good. Therefore, if we have lived according to the form of life given us, we shall, by very little effort, leave others a noble example and gain the prize of eternal happiness (TC6).

The fidelity and authenticity of our commitment, manifested in community, provides a model for those in the world of what a life with God can mean and demonstrates to them the possibilities of their own hearts to strive for holiness.

Directly or indirectly St. Clare refers to a number of qualities or characteristics necessary for this life in community to achieve its objectives. The outer or tangible forms of community living express and bring about the inner or hid-

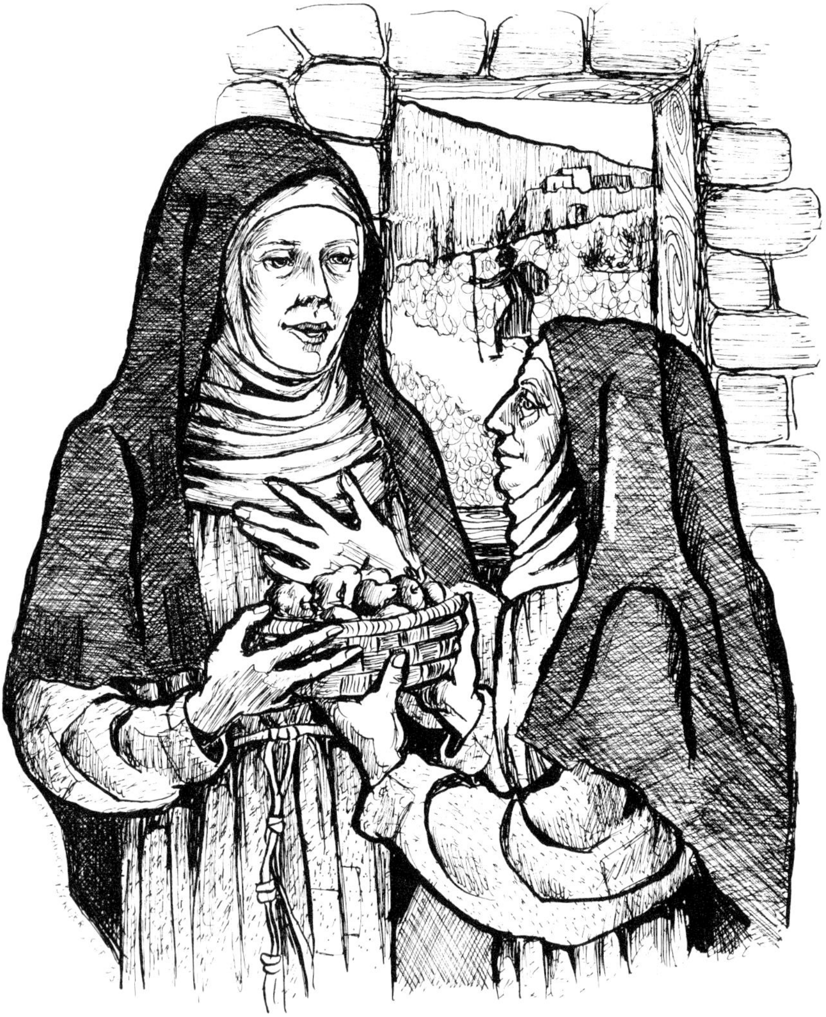

den reality of the community's meaning and ministry to become the icon of the gentleness of God.

The first quality is a *lived experience of togetherness* (that "unity of mutual love" (RC10:5) which Clare talks about). The *Franciscan* style of community is different from the traditions of other spiritual families in the Church. It is not a togetherness based on the hierarchy and stability of cenobitic family life (Benedictine), nor the "common life" of Augustinians or Dominicans, nor the uniformity of observances of Norbertines or Croziers or other clerics regular, nor the united work force for the apostolate (more contemporary congregations). Rather, the raison d'etre is precisely the commitment of persons to persons in order to manifest a common attachment to the same poor and crucified Christ, a collective liberation from earthly attachments, a corporate witness to the gentleness of God. The implications of this quality for life in community are as follows:

a) Community is a gift to be discovered and lived out; it is dependent upon the urgings of grace and the demands of God's initiative, and not just upon one's own categories of acceptance, whims of decision, or choice of partners.

b) Community is based upon a free and responsible acceptance of a call; it is togetherness because of personal self-giving, willful decision, and the obligation flowing from intimacy, not just legislation or communal structures. It is a concrete expression of "one body, one spirit in Christ," the being of "one mind and one heart," not a togetherness based upon regular observance or uniformity.

c) Community life has to reflect the Father's loving us intensely, his choosing us to come together in Jesus Christ, his giving the energy of the Holy Spirit to restore all things in Christ.

d) Life in community recognizes the dignity of every person to be a chosen child of God, to be redeemed by Christ, to have the potential to respond to the Spirit's urging, to be the artisan of one's own world, to embody a unique blend of characteristics or talents.

The second quality of community is the delicate *balance between leadership and obedience* to "preserve the unity of mutual love and peace" (RC 4:16). On the one hand, Clare points out how absolutely necessary it is for the abbess to be lovingly solicitous and caring toward her sisters in order to promote mutual love: "She should console those who are afflicted, and be, likewise, the last refuge for those who are disturbed. ... She should preserve the common life in everything" (RC4:9,10). Moreover, "[r]egarding the sisters who are ill, the Abbess is strictly bound to inquire with all solicitude by herself and through other sisters what these sick sisters may need both by way of counsel and of food and other necessities and, according to the resources of the place, she is to provide for them charitably and kindly" (RC8:7).

In her Testament Clare fondly describes the characteristics of a loving abbess:

> I also beg that sister who will have the office of caring for the sisters to strive to exceed others more by her virtue and holy life than by her office so that, encouraged by her example, the Sisters may obey her not so much out of duty but rather out of love. Let her also be prudent and attentive to her sisters just as a good mother is to her daughters; and especially, let her take care to provide for them according to the needs of each one from the things which the Lord shall give. Let her also be so kind and so available that all of them may reveal their needs with trust and have recourse to her at any hour with confidence as they see fit, both for her sake and that of her sisters (TC19).

On the other hand, Clare emphasizes that the form of life is to observe the holy Gospel by living in obedience (RC1:3); that profession is to "be received into obedience" (RC2:7). She is quick to profess her obedience to the Church (TC13), to the Pope (RC1:3), to the Cardinal Protector (TC13), and to Francis and his successors the Ministers General (RC1:4, TC14). This obedience is not just a bending of will or a virtue of abandonment, but rather an act of love. If the Lord is present in the Church and if God's graciousness and gentleness are present in the community, then those in authority who duly represent the Church and the Order are icons or sacraments or representations of the loving and tender and solicitous presence of God Himself. Therefore, one responds to that presence not out of fear nor out of duty, but rather out of love and out of an eagerness to return the love received.

Clare expresses this special interaction between authority and obedience when she says:

> The Abbess should admonish and visit her sisters, and humbly and charitably correct them, not commanding them anything which would be against their soul and the form of our profession. The sisters, however, who are subjects, should remember that for God's sake they have renounced their own wills. Hence, they are firmly bound to obey their Abbess in all things which they promise the Lord to observe and which are not against their soul and our profession. On her part, the Abbess is to be so familiar with them that they can speak and act toward her as ladies do with their servant. For that is the way it should be, that the Abbess be the servant of all the sisters (RC10:1-3).

The next quality of life in community is the *development of persons* which is expressed in various media:

a) formation which gives meaning and purpose to human life: "The Abbess shall carefully provide a Mistress from among the more prudent sisters of the monastery both for these and the other novices. She shall form them diligently in a holy manner of living and proper behavior according to the form of our profession" (RC2:14).

b) praying for each other and praying in common: "Let us pray to God together for each other for, by sharing each other's burden of charity in this way, we shall easily fulfill the law of Christ" (LE17); and "The Sisters who can read shall celebrate the Divine Office..." (RC3:1ff).

c) the support and direction of understanding and pardon: "The Abbess and her sisters must beware not to become angry or disturbed on account of anyone's sin: for anger and disturbance prevent charity in oneself and in others" (RC9:3); and "The other sister, mindful of that word of the Lord: If you do not forgive from the heart, neither will your heavenly Father forgive you, should generously pardon her sister every wrong she has done her" (RC9:5).

d) using the means of dialogue and trust to overcome any problematic situation: "Each should make known her needs to the other with confidence. For if a mother loves and nourishes her daughter according to the flesh, how much more lovingly must a sister love and nourish her sister according to the Spirit!" (RC8:9).

e) the exercise of personal integrity: "In the Lord Jesus Christ, I admonish and exhort all my sisters, both present and those to come, to strive always to imitate the way of holy simplicity, humility, and poverty and to preserve the integrity of our holy manner of life, as we were taught by our blessed Father Francis from the beginning of our conversion to Christ. Thus may they always remain in the fragrance of a good name, both among those who are afar off and those who are near" (TC17).

The last quality of community life, sprinkled throughout all of Clare's writing, is the *practical sustaining forces* which nourish life together and make it work. These are the gatherings of the community (prayer, meals, chapters, retreats, common work, recreation, etc.); the many and varied sustenance factors (spiritually, psychologically, materially) from a library for spiritual reading to games to be played in common to donations and fruits of the community's labor; and the concrete efforts to preserve and promote the uniqueness and the communality of the Franciscan-Clarian charism (like interaction with other members of the Franciscan Family or participation in workshops or institutes).

With this kind of community life the gentleness of God is made manifest which, along with God's graciousness shown through poverty and refreshment expressed in contemplation, makes real the loving initiative of the Lord, discovered through discernment, to inflame the heart of the beloved through penance, chastity, and constancy and to empower the beloved to mirror and relive and communicate that love for all to behold.

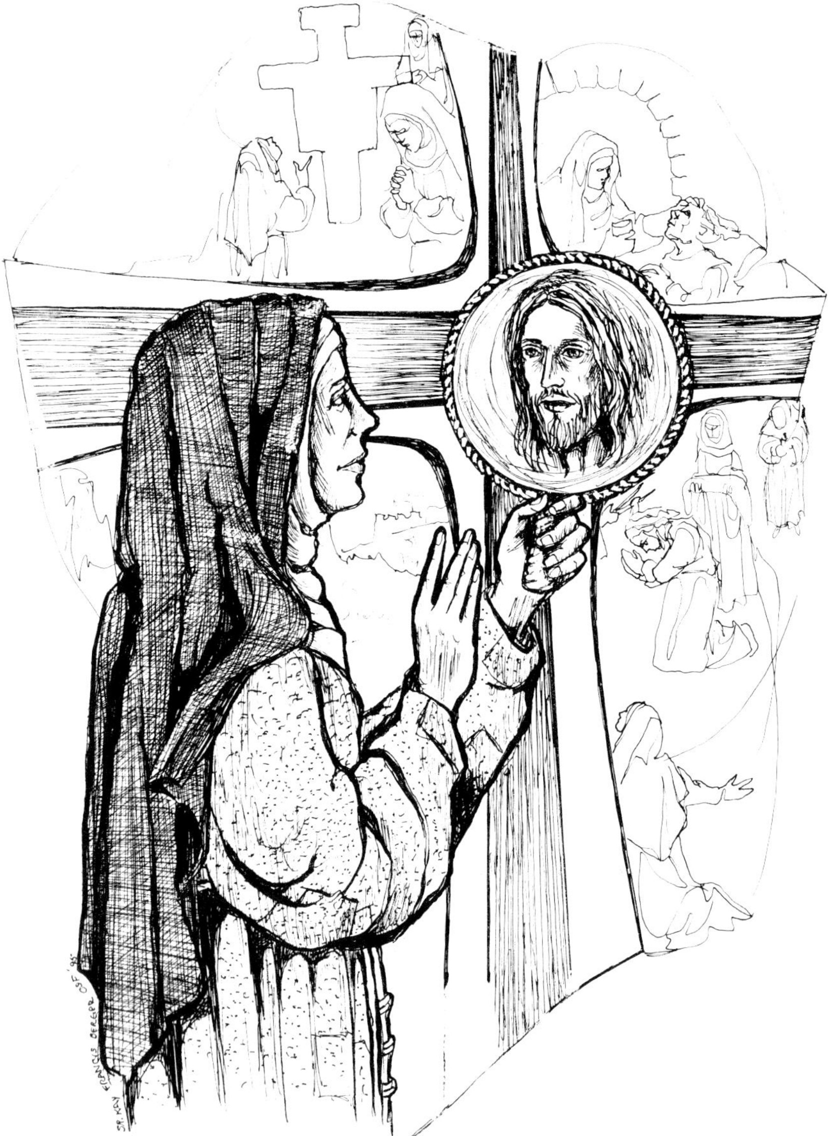

chapter six

"Models and Mirrors for Others" (TC8)

St. Clare had a keen sense of the impact of her sisters' life and spirituality upon other people, both in the Church and in the world. She was well aware that her way of life was not only directed toward achieving holiness and striving for intimate union with God, but also existed for the good of the Body of Christ and for the well-being of the world. Her own words at the end of her life give witness to this fact:

> With what solicitude and fervor of mind and body, therefore, must we keep the commandments of our God and Father, so that, with the help of the Lord, we may return to Him an increase of His talents. For the Lord Himself not only has set us as an example and mirror for others, but also for our own sisters whom the Lord has called to our way of life, so that they in turn will be a mirror and example to those living in the world. Since, therefore, the Lord has called us to such great things, that those who are to be models and mirrors for others may behold themselves in us, we are truly bound to bless and praise the Lord and

to be strengthened constantly in Him to do good. Therefore, if we have lived according to the form of life given us, we shall, by very little effort, leave others a noble example and gain the prize of eternal happiness (TC6).

Clare's own testimony gives witness to the words of Jesus to his disciples: "The gift you have received, give as a gift" (Mt 10:8), and "your light must shine before all so that they may see goodness in your acts and give praise to your heavenly Father" (Mt 5:16).

Clare, "the unworthy handmaid of Christ and the little plant of the most blessed Father Francis" (RC1:3), the poor and penitential contemplative, the faithful virgin living in mutual love with her sisters, was a true evangelizer. That precious vocation of hers was to proclaim the presence of Christ as well as to interact with It intimately. The Love she received she shared, the Light she encountered she mirrored, the Life she experienced she witnessed.

As we will see from our continued study of her words to Agnes of Prague, this effort at evangelization took on three interconnected yet slightly different modes: mirroring the poor and crucified Christ, witnessing to the revivification (new life) brought about by one's self-giving (kenosis), and communicating the vision of happiness (Good News) to all she encounters.

"Whose Remembrance Brings a Gentle Light"

To remember is to make present. For Clare the bringing to mind and the making present of the poor and crucified Christ, her Lover and Beloved, her Mentor and Model, her Motivation and her Master, was a source of intense but gentle light which illumined her whole existence and elucidated the meaning and purpose of all she was and did. The image she is

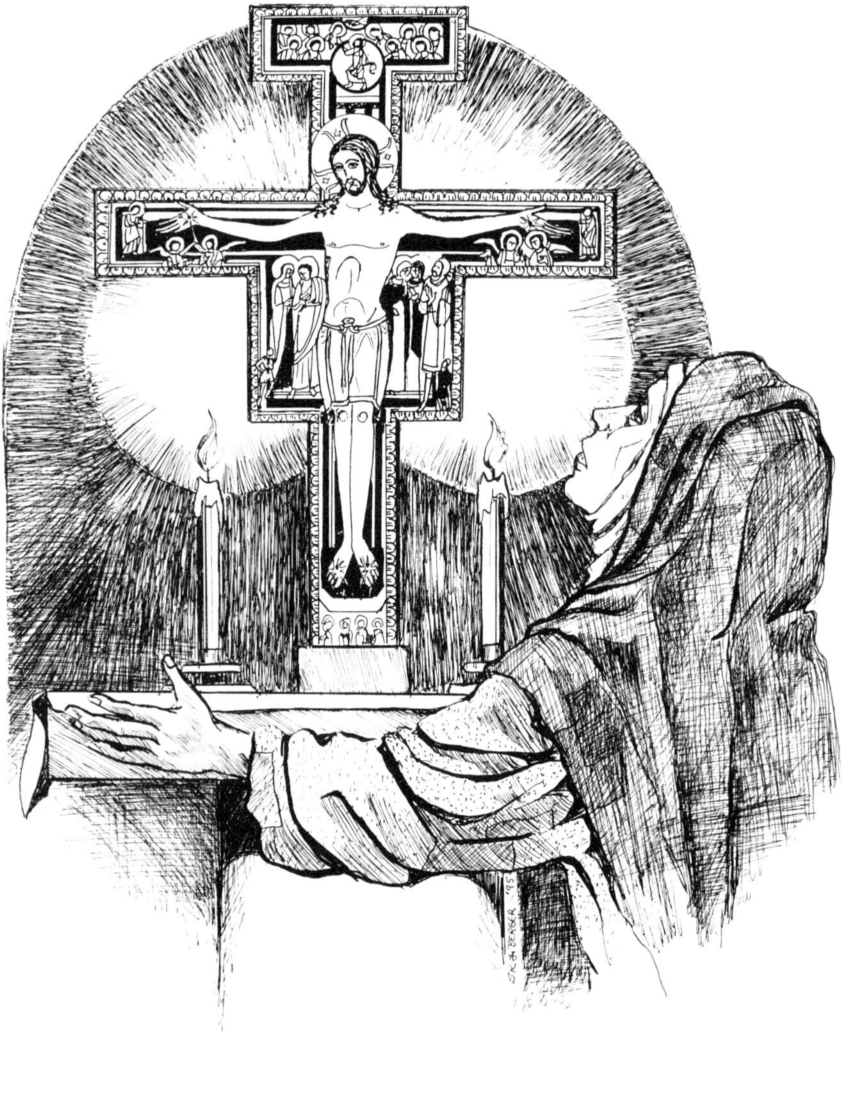

accustomed to use to describe this experience is that of the "mirror":

> Place your mind before the mirror of eternity!
> Place your soul in the brilliance of glory!
> Place your heart in the figure of the divine
>   substance!
> And transform your whole being into the
>   image of the Godhead Itself
>   through contemplation!
> So that you too may feel what His friends feel
>   as they taste the hidden sweetness
>   which God himself has reserved
>   from the beginning
>   for those who love him (3L12-14).

This encounter with the Mirror had, actually, a threefold purpose: the revelation of Christ, the uncovering of oneself because of this revelation, and the mirroring of this revelation to others because of one's authenticity.

When a person looks into a mirror, what is seen is the reflection of that very person. With Clare this reality had a dual application: First of all, being filled with the presence of Christ, having the Blessed Trinity dwell within, and identifying with the poor and crucified Christ put her in the position of encountering the reflection of the Lord Jesus in the mirror of life's experiences. Because of the shape of the medieval mirror and its propensity to have more clarity toward the center and less clarity on the edges, she is able to describe this imaging at great length:

> Inasmuch as this vision is the splendor of
> eternal glory, the brilliance of eternal light
> and the mirror without blemish, look upon
> that mirror each day, O queen and spouse of
> Jesus Christ, and continually study your face

within it, so that you may adorn yourself within and without with beautiful robes and cover yourself with the flowers and garments of all the virtues, as becomes the daughter and most chaste bride of the Most High King. Indeed, blessed poverty, holy humility, and ineffable charity are reflected in that mirror, as, with the grace of God, you can contemplate them throughout the entire mirror.

Look at the parameters of this mirror, that is, the poverty of Him Who was placed in a manger and wrapped in swaddling clothes. O marvelous humility, O astonishing poverty! The King of the angels, the Lord of heaven and earth, is laid in a manger! Then, at the surface of the mirror, dwell on the holy humility, the blessed poverty, the untold labors and burdens which He endured for the redemption of the whole human race. Then, in the depths of this same mirror, contemplate the ineffable charity which led Him to suffer on the wood of the Cross and die thereon the most shameful kind of death. Therefore, that Mirror, suspended on the wood of the Cross, urged those who passed by to consider, saying: "All you who pass by the way, look and see if there is any suffering like My suffering!" Let us answer Him with one voice and spirit, as He said: Remembering this over and over leaves my soul downcast within me. From this moment, then, O queen of our heavenly King, let yourself be inflamed more strongly with the fervor of charity (4L14-27).

Through the parameters of the mirror—life all around

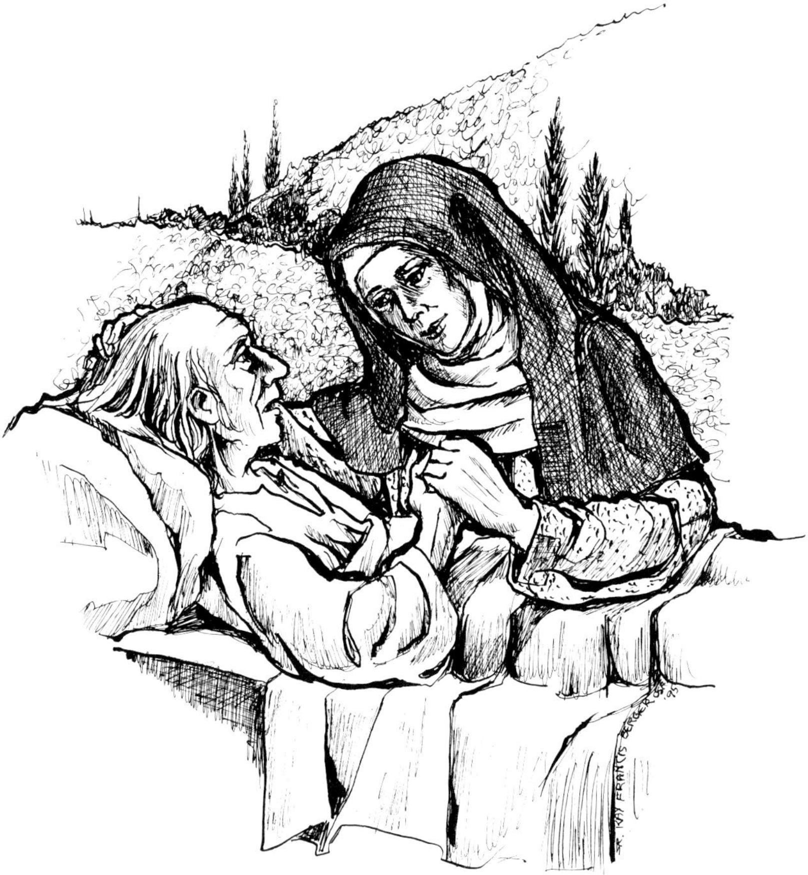

her socially, politically, economically, ecclesiastically—she comes in touch with the Word made flesh and dwelling along us. On the surface of the mirror—the history of her own personal experiences—she encounters the redemptive experience of Jesus in her regard: how he called her, betrothed her, brought her into the chamber of his own poverty and humility. In the depth of the mirror—the penance and contemplation and charity of her own heart—she is overwhelmed by the beauty of Light itself, the "ineffable charity" of the one who gave himself completely that she might live.

This mirror experience of Christ uncovers the reality of herself. She evaluates her own response to the Incarnation in the people she has met, in the events she has gone through, in the difficulties she has endured. She critiques the intensity of her own efforts to say "yes" to the Lover who beckons and the Beloved who avails Himself to her by means of her poverty and penance, her chastity and commitment to community. She reflects on the quality of her own self-giving in contemplation vis-a-vis the kenosis of Christ.

The scenario of the mirror, however, does not stop here. Because of her encounter with Christ and because of her own self-awareness owing to that exchange of love, she is able to mirror to others for all ages the reality of a relationship with the poor and crucified Christ. The clarity of her experience and the authenticity of her response become a source of evangelization for the whole world. She witnesses to the Church what intimacy with Christ really is. She shows to the world how important life with God must be and how empty life is without it.

"Whose Fragrance Will Revive the Dead"

Clare's work of evangelization also operates as "smelling salts" for those who have become faint in their God-orientation, as a "fragrance" to revive those of dying spirits. Her life and her spirituality give witness to the new life of resurrection—a revitalization or a revivification or a rejuvenation of a spiritual journey.

Clare's premise is simple and straightforward: Christ is Life ("I am the Way, the Truth, and the Life; no one comes to the Father but through me" {Jn 14:6}). He came to bring life ("I came that they might have life and have it to the full" {Jn 10:10}). If we unite with him, we share life ("I am the vine, you are the branches. He who lives in me and I in him, will produce abundantly, for apart from me you can do nothing" {Jn 15:5}). If we share his life, we live ("Whoever believes in the Son has life eternal" {Jn 3:36}, and "If a person is true to my word, that one shall never see death" {Jn 8:51}). When we live, we spark the hearts of others, cause them to evaluate their life situation, and by the grace of God bring them to embrace life too ("As the Father has loved me, so I have loved you. Live on in my love. ... This is my commandment: love one another as I have loved you" {Jn 15:9,12}).

Clare indicates, then, that fidelity to the gospel life in all its dimensions is not only a source of new life for the sisters themselves:

> Because of this you shall share always and forever the glory of the kingdom of heaven in place of earthly and passing things, and everlasting treasures instead of those that perish, and you shall live forever (2L23).

but also is a means for communicating that very same life to others (i.e., evangelization):

> On earth, may He increase His grace and virtues among His servants and handmaids of His Church Militant. In heaven, may He exalt and glorify you in His Church Triumphant among all His men and women saints (BC8-9).

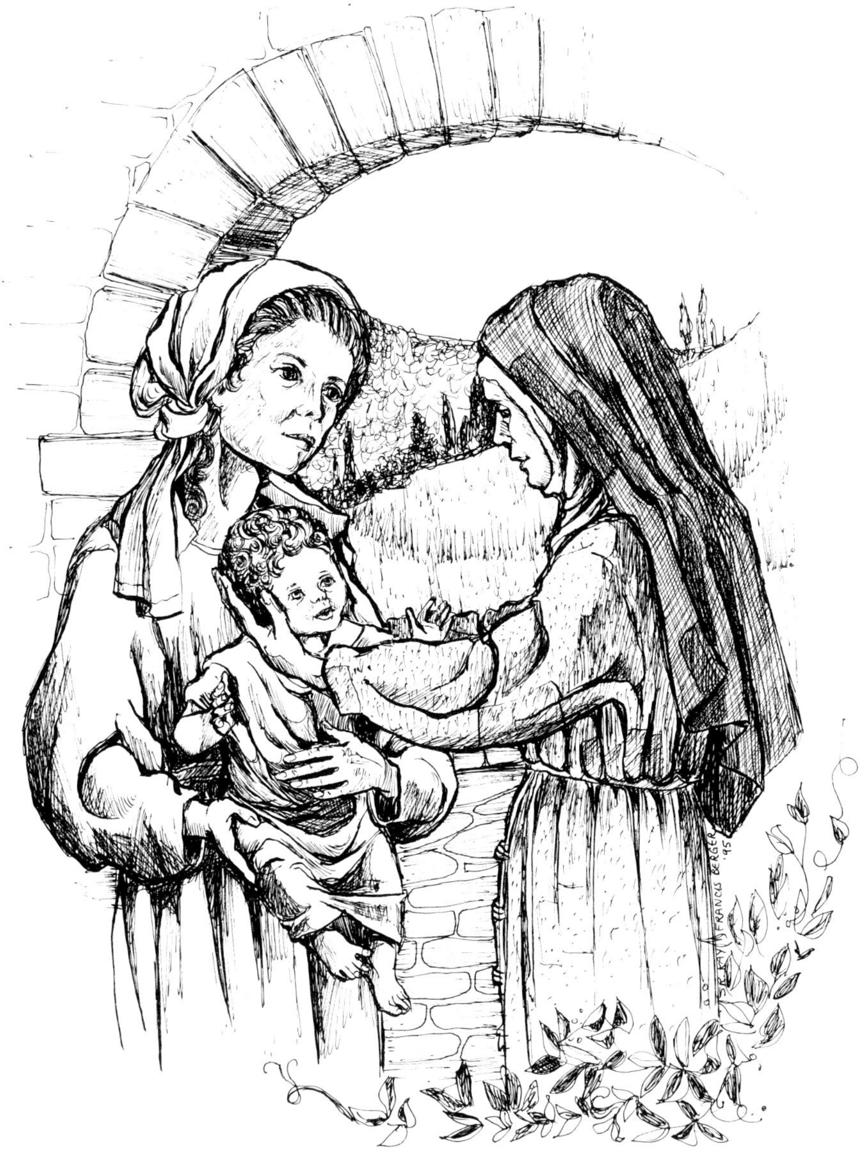
SR. KAY FRANCIS BERGER '95

"Whose Glorious Vision Will Be the Happiness of All the Citizens of the Heavenly Jerusalem"

Finally, Clare's evangelizing efforts include the communication of the glorious vision of the Blessed Trinity through prayer and example so that this presence to others will bring about a depth of peace and joy which can be experienced nowhere else.

Clare saw the power of intercessory prayer as a means of evangelization:

> I also beg You in the Lord, as much as I can, to include in Your holy prayers me, Your servant, though unworthy, and the other sisters with me in the monastery, who are all devoted to You, so that by their help we may merit the mercy of Jesus Christ, and together with You may merit to enjoy the everlasting vision (1L33-34).

If the sisters—who have come to experience the intense and intimate presence of the Lord through their penance and poverty and their contemplation and life in community—intercede with their Beloved that this same vision be shared with others, then it will happen insofar as the one receiving the power of intercessory prayer is open to the Vision of Beauty gifted by the Lord himself. This is why, from the time of Clare herself, the Poor Ladies of the cloister were asked to pray for specific people and for particular intentions, so that the "glorious vision" of the Lord will make happy the hearts of those being prayed for.

Moreover, the example of charity on the part of the sisters also shares this holy and awesome vision because of the transparency of their own authenticity of vocation:

Only the faithful soul is His dwelling place and His throne, and this is possible only through the charity which the wicked do not have. He Who is Truth has said: Whoever loves me will be loved by My Father, and I too shall love him, and We shall come to him and make our dwelling place with Him. Therefore, as the glorious Virgin of virgins carried Christ materially in her body, you, too, by following in His footprints, especially those of poverty and humility, can, without any doubt, always carry him spiritually in your chaste and virginal body. And you will hold Him by Whom you and all things are held together, thus possessing that which, in comparison with the other transitory possessions of this world, you will possess more securely" (3L22-26).

In other words, when the sisters reveal the story of God working in their lives, are filled with this vision, and possess this reality now because of their fidelity and honesty in living out the various aspects of their vocation, then their living testimony of peace and joy activates the hearts and minds, the attitudes and behavior of others to tell the story all over again and achieve a similar happiness. Their witness prompts inspiration and imitation, their example prompts motivation and modeling. Their being evangelized becomes a source of evangelization for others.

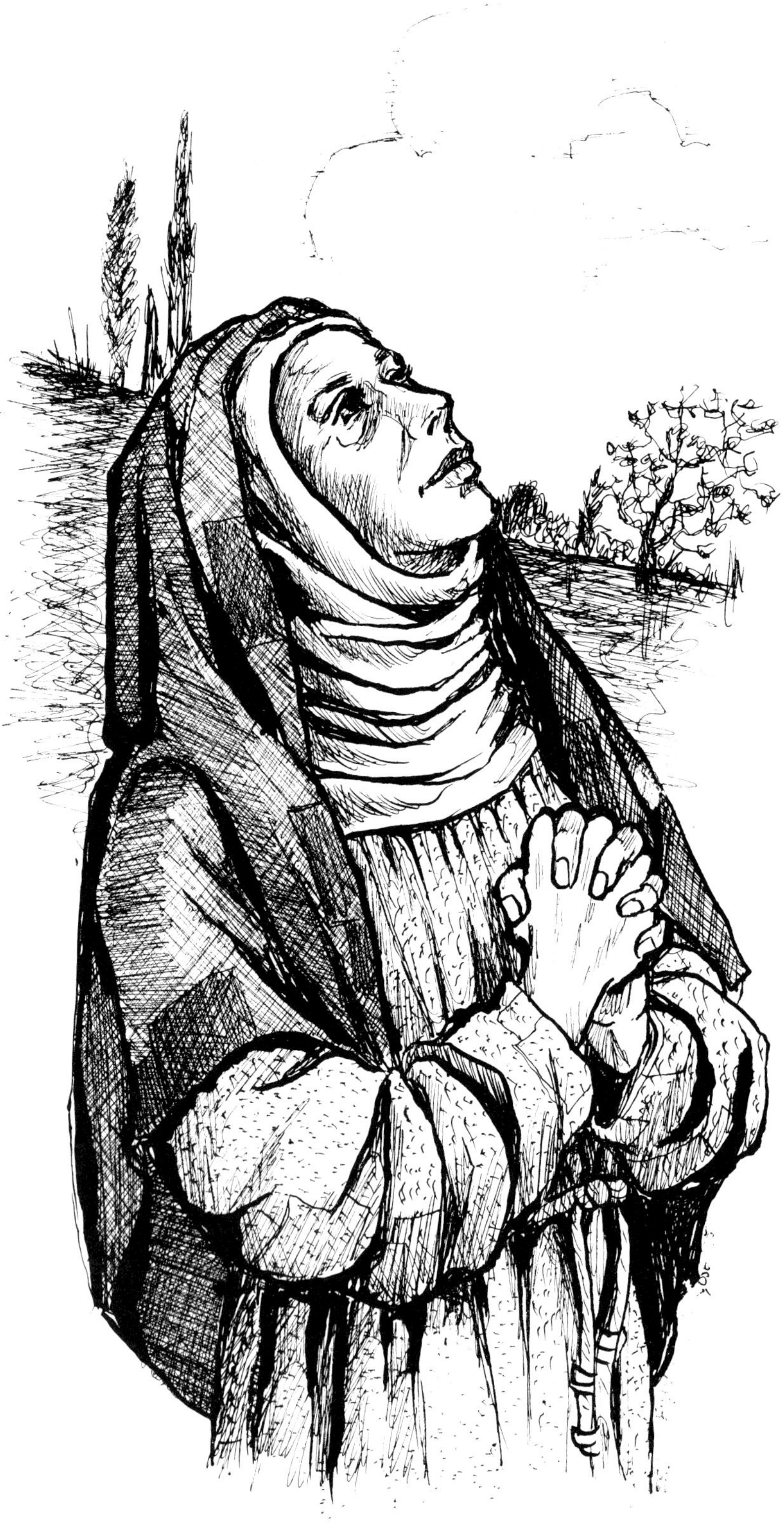

Conclusion

St. Clare's goal in life was to "cling with all her heart to Him" who loved her and called her and gifted her with blessedness so that she could "share this sacred banquet" of the reign of God in her life (cf. 4L9). The experience of her spiritual journey toward this goal led her to describe her lifestyle as admiring the beauty of God's enlightenment through discernment; returning the love she experienced through ongoing conversion, chastity, and constancy; being refreshed in this love encounter through contemplation; coming to know the graciousness of God through poverty; touching the gentleness of God by means of life in community; and making present the awesome vision and glorious remembrance and pleasing fragrance of this awesome experience by mirroring Christ's revelation, witnessing to his new life, and becoming a powerful example for others.

This spirituality was not Clare's alone, not just the property of her sisters. It is a treasure for the worldwide Franciscan Family (friars, nuns, seculars, brothers and sisters alike), a gift to the whole Church, and a valuable resource for all people of good will.

The concluding word, then, is the admonition and prayer of St. Bonaventure (as related in his Second Letter):

> May you walk earnestly in the footprints of your holy Mother Clare who, through the instrumentality of the little poor man Saint Francis, was schooled by the Holy Spirit.

Endnotes:

1. The quotes from the Writings of St. Clare are taken from *Francis and Clare: The Complete Works* by Regis Armstrong OFMCap and Ignatius Brady OFM (New York: Paulist Press, 1982). The abbreviations for the writings are as follows:
   - 1L = First Letter to Agnes of Prague
   - 2L = Second Letter to Agnes of Prague
   - 3L = Third Letter to Agnes of Prague
   - 4L = Fourth Letter to Agnes of Prague
   - LE = Letter to Ermentrude of Bruges
   - RC = Rule of St. Clare
   - TC = Testament of St. Clare
   - BC = Blessing of St. Clare

   The number following the name indicates the numbered sentence of the particular text.

2. Susan Muto's presentation given at "Clarefest '93" in LaCrosse, Wisconsin, June 3-6, 1993, gave me the inspiration for this basic outline of St. Clare's spirituality. To her I am indebted and very grateful.